Creating Life On Our Own Terms

Dr Angela C. Robertson

Creating Life On Our Own Terms

Paradise Publishing 2021

Disclaimer: This collection of personal stories was written in consultation with the individuals concerned and is published with their consent. The contents are the personal views of each individual and as such the author and publisher disclaim any liability in connection with the use of this information or for issues of fact or interpretation. Neither the author, nor the publisher accept referral fees or commissions from individuals or companies that may be mentioned in this publication.

ISBN: 978-0-9951371-4-1

Cover Image:

Steven Novak Novakillustrations.com

Books by the same author
in the *'Older and Bolder'* series

Available online from your favourite bookstores

Life On Our Own Terms

ISBN: 978-0-473-50082-5 Paperback

Celebrating Life On Our Own Terms

ISBN: 978-0-473-51912-4 Paperback

Embracing Life On Our Own Terms

ISBN: 978-0-995-1371-2-7 Paperback

CONTENTS

Preface

1 Introduction — Pg 1

2 Jennie Sherwin — Pg 3

3 John Skene — Pg 16

4 Gaylene Denford-Wood — Pg 25

5 Kevin Boyce — Pg 37

6 Jim and Dereley Barry — Pg 56

7 Mike Elliott — Pg 66

8 Solveig Mikkelsen — Pg 79

9 Maureen Taylor — Pg 91

10 Alison Merwood — Pg102

11 Ken Allan — Pg111

12 Helen Dew — Pg120

13 Jim and Joan Bolger — Pg130

14 Jim Gibson — Pg146

15 Andy Higham — Pg152

16 Jean Douglas — Pg162

17 June Rowland   Pg171

18 Afterthoughts   Pg181

19 About the Author   Pg184

"Life is what you make it, has been, always will be"

Eleanor Roosevelt

PREFACE

The inspiration for the Older and Bolder series of books came from chatting with dozens of men and women who range in age from their mid-50's to 100+ years. While each of their life stories are unique, they share some common threads. In the second half of life, they challenge the stereotypical belief that advancing age narrows down life choices. Their attitudes to life and their perspective on ageing is both insightful and inspirational. The collection of cameo life stories captured in this fourth book in the series, were documented in the midst of the COVID pandemic. In these challenging times, these individuals, who all live in New Zealand, appreciate how lucky we are, and are optimistic about the future. It has been a privilege to have met these awesome men and women. It's with their permission that a lifetime of wildly different backgrounds, experiences and perspectives can be shared with you. Accepting that we all age differently, these individuals show us that whatever our age and circumstances, later life has the potential to be even more productive and fulfilling than what has gone before. Despite the curve balls many of us experience, these individuals continue to move out of their comfort zones, are expanding their horizons, and take advantage of the opportunities around them. They create their reality, and inspired by their example, so can we!

"We are the creative force of our life, and through our decisions rather than our conditions"

Stephen Covey

INTRODUCTION

Globally the population is ageing. With increased life expectancy, and dramatic improvements in health care, we are enjoying extended lifespans. Annually, centenarians, semi-centenarians (people aged between 105-109 years), and super-centenarians (those aged 110 and over), are growing in numbers. In New Zealand, it's expected a fifth of the population will be over the age of 65 by 2034, (Better Later Life He Oranga Kaumatua 2019 to 2034 msd.govt.nz).

The potential to live longer and healthier lives creates new life stages, opportunities, and exciting challenges for everyone. This is changing our perspective on ageing. In New Zealand, there is no official retirement age, although there are a few exceptions. Those over the age of 65, who meet the legal requirements, may be eligible for New Zealand superannuation - whether or not they are still working. Given the changing demographic it's not unusual for more than one generation in families to be eligible for superannuation. Regardless, nearly one in four people, over the age of 65, choose to remain in the workplace, on either a part-time or fulltime basis for a variety of reasons, and this number is growing. Others, having reached this stage in their lives choose to change direction – to start a new career or small business; to undertake new projects or activities they had previously never considered, or perhaps only dreamt about. What does later life look like for you? Are you working, retired, or somewhere in between? Are you looking toward the future with apprehension or excitement?

Mid-life for many is a time for reflection. It's one of those phases in life when we take stock of what we've experienced to date, what we've achieved, and who and what is important to us. The second half of life is an opportunity to re-vision and re-ignite our lives. Accepting that we all age differently, given the gift of healthier extended lifespans, it makes sense to embrace the ageing process, take good care of ourselves, enjoy life's pleasures, and make the most of the additional years later life offers. We all face circumstances that may be beyond our control, but as Napoleon Hill, author of 'Think and Grow Rich' once said, "Our only limitations are the ones we set up in our own minds". We create our own reality, and we can do that at any age. After all, our chronological age is just a number, and many believe it's a state of mind. We can take advantage of the opportunities that are all around us, if we open our minds to the possibilities, and move out of our comfort zones.

We all love stories and can learn from other people's experience. The individuals you'll meet in this book are from all walks of life. During our conversations I captured the context of their earlier lives, their aspirations, plans, and perspectives, their resilience in the face of adversity, and documented the choices they made that shaped their future. In their 60's, 70's 80's and 90's they demonstrate that, depending on one's mindset, whatever your age and circumstances, later life has the potential to be even more productive and fulfilling than what has gone before. It's a privilege to share their cameo stories with you in this fourth book in the 'Older and Bolder' series. These individuals create life on their own terms, and without exception make the most of what life has to offer.

Let me introduce you to them.

JENNIE SHERWIN

Jennie and her husband Peter met on a blind date arranged by the Receptionist at Barr, Burgess and Stewart for their annual Christmas function. At the time, Peter (then aged 22) and Jennie (who was 19) were students. They had both been doing work experience with this firm in Palmerston North. Peter was studying to be a Chartered Accountant at Victoria University and Jennie was undertaking a secretarial course at the Polytechnic. Jennie recalls, "Peter drove all the way from Palmerston North to my family home in Feilding to pick me up". From the onset they got on really well together. The relationship blossomed and two years later they tied the knot at St John's Anglican Church in Feilding, just two weeks after Jennie's 21st birthday.

When they completed their studies, Peter and Jennie secured permanent jobs at Barr, Burgess and Stewart where they worked for a further two years. When the couple moved to Wellington, they bought a home in Papakowhai. Peter's career went from strength to strength when he went into partnership with McKissack and Andrew. Later, he took over this business and was able to put everything he had learned into practice. Jennie worked in accounts for a communications company and an interior decorating company but knew she wanted to channel her energy into something completely different.

Changing direction, Jennie bought 'Etro', a clothing store in the Harbour City Centre that specialised in mature women's apparel. She quickly learned everything about running a small retail business and chose all of the stock from several reputable Auckland suppliers. Jennie just loved the business and was totally absorbed in developing it when, after years of trying, she found she was pregnant with their first child. Although thrilled with the news, Jennie was torn between giving up the business and becoming a stay-at-home Mum or keeping the business and bringing their baby son Martin to work with her. She chose the latter. For six-months Martin went to work with his Mum several times a week, and at nap times, slept in the pram in the back room. Jennie found it difficult to juggle both roles simultaneously, and this was further hampered by the 1987 economic crash that had a huge impact on retail trade. Six months later Jennie decided to sell her stock, give away the lease, close her business and focus on her family. Their second child, Natalie, was born in 1991. Jennie loved being a full-time stay-at-home Mum raising their two pre-schoolers and supported Peter in his business.

Within a few years, Peter and Jennie began to look for a larger home for their growing family on a life-style block within commuting distance to Wellington. They found the perfect property 22 kilometres north of Wellington in Whitby - a two-and-a-half-acre section, that had a woolshed they planned to convert into a small cottage that they would live in. This would be an interim step before taking on a bigger project to design and build their forever home. Recognising the potential, Jennie and Peter were excited about taking on these projects. It took the couple two years to convert the woolshed into a family home. "We had never taken on a project like this before, and we loved every minute of it", said Jennie. "By the time we moved in, Martin was six years old, and Natalie was three".

No sooner had they moved into the cottage than work began on their second project to build a much bigger family home in front of the cottage. As they were living on the property, this building project took less time to construct before they could move in (10 months), and they did much of the painting and finishing touches themselves. Now, nearly 30 years later, the couple still live in their forever home and rent their cottage to their long-term tenants.

While the children were growing up Jennie pursued several creative art and craft projects in her spare time. She had always knitted and sewed and later became interested in batik whereby she applied her artwork to textiles using dye resistance techniques. Realising she really enjoyed creative crafts, and wanting to learn more, she signed up for several artistic courses at the local polytechnic. She took pottery, ceramics and print making classes, and learned how to use colour. In her early 40's she had found her passion and wanted to learn more and more. Extending her artistic skills, she took up tapestry and cross stitch and began to paint on zincalume – aluminium, zinc, and silicon corrugated metal. These were crafts she could work on at home. Inspired by a love of nature, Jennie's artwork mainly focused on this theme, especially flowers and birds. Peter was very supportive and made the wooden frames for her zincalume paintings, some of which were up to a square metre in size! Encouraged by the feedback from family and friends, Jennie began to sell her art at the weekend markets. This was so successful she set up a cottage industry that she ran from home and extended her range of products using acrylic.

When the children grew up and left home, Jennie turned her hand to making contemporary jewellery, specifically big jewellery. Self-taught, she followed her creative instinct. She purchased the beading supplies online and using carefully selected stones, built-in colour wherever the inspiration led her. Jennie sold her jewellery range at the markets.

In the late 1980's, the World of Wearable Art was a relatively new concept. It was initiated by Sculptor Suzie Moncrieff, who proposed that art could be hung on the human form, not just the wall. The first World of Wearable (WOW) Art show was held in a community hall in Nelson. Approximately 200 people attended, and from there the idea really took off and WOW became an annual event. One day, Jennie and her friend spotted an advertisement for one of these events on a public noticeboard in Porirua and her girlfriend said, "We could do that"! The idea took hold. For the next five years Jennie, inspired by nature, designed and created full-scale costumes for the competition. Each of these costumes took months of work to create, and all of them had to meet the criteria for the categories she had selected in the competition. The following is a list of the creations that Jennie submitted within the various categories.

- 1997   Avante Garde Section – *"Four Seasons"*
- 1998   Children's Section - *"There are fairies in my garden"*.
- 1999   Natural Forces - *"The Eruption of Man's Destruction"*.
- 2000   Avante Garde Section - *"Desert Dweller"*.

Once made, the costumes had to be transported to Nelson, where a panel of judges selected the "most innovative and outstanding entries that would appear on stage in that year's World of Wearable Arts Show", which at the time was held in Nelson. Disappointingly, over that five-year period, none of

Jennie's original designs were chosen by the judges. Jennie asked herself, "What am I doing wrong"?

Seeking help, Jennie approached Kate O'Byrne, a neurolinguistic programming practitioner. Jennie said, "Kate was so helpful. She introduced me to the concept of guided imagery. Using this technique, she guided me through several creative visualisations. In each one I was able to visualise a garment in great detail. In my mind's eye, one particular garment stood out. It was a giant sea urchin. In the guided visualisation I could see all of the parts of this artistic project and could even describe the multi coloured spines. It was an amazing experience"! Following this session with Kate, Jennie, inspired by the experience, made several drawings, sketching out what her creation "Kina-A-Delic Surprise (Sea Urchin)" would look like. Then she got to work to put it together using wood for the frame and glow in the dark fabric in white and fluro colours for its multicoloured spines.

It took months to create this masterpiece that would be submitted in the Illumination Illusion Section for the next World of Wearable Arts show. When completed, the Sea Urchin was so big it needed to be put on a trailer to be transported. Jennie said, "I drove it into Wellington myself to be loaded onto the ferry to Picton, and from there it would go on to Nelson in time to arrive well before the show". In 2000, her innovative, original creation was accepted by the judges for the very first time. Jennie was thrilled. This was such an achievement. Leading up to the World of Wearable Art event, Jennie and all of her family headed to Nelson for the show. When the big day came, they were amazed when they saw Jennie's garment at the show, "It was so big, I was so proud, as was all of my family"!

Fired up with enthusiasm, the following year Jennie teamed up with friend Margie du Bern to work on a joint project. Their creation was made with organza and silk fabric and decorated with more than 300 pieces of paua shell sewn on to the bodice. Their costume, named "Sea Seduction", was submitted in the Oceania Section. After months of work the women were overjoyed when their submission was selected by the judges for the 2001 World of Wearable Art Show.

In 2008 Jennie submitted two exhibits in the Bizarre Bra Section - "See Cup" and "Flat Chested", and a costume in the Children's Section called "Two Two Tutus". Disappointingly, none of the submissions were successful.

Meanwhile, Jennie's daughter Natalie also had an idea for an exhibit for WOW. Natalie's idea was actually called 'WOW' whereby models dressed in black, joined together – each one with their outer arm, when open, displayed a 'W' on it, and the 'O' was in the middle. This incredibly creative garment was accepted in the Illumination Section. At the time, Natalie was the youngest of the applicants to get in! It was a very proud moment for the family.

Overall, Jennie entered the World of Wearable Arts competition ten times, creating an original design each time. On reflection she said, "There was so much personal satisfaction of being part of something like this". From its humble beginnings, over these years the World of Wearable Arts, became an internationally recognised design competition that now attracts entries from designers all over the world. The annual event was later moved from Nelson to Wellington to accommodate the thousands of people that now attend these shows each year.

Creating Life On Our Own Terms

"There are fairies in my garden" – modelled by daughter Natalie

"Kina-A-Delic Surprise (Sea Urchin)" – Photo taken at Pauatahanui

"Sea Seduction" modelled by Karen Carpenter.
Photo taken by the Evening Post on the beach at Pauatahanui

Creating Life On Our Own Terms

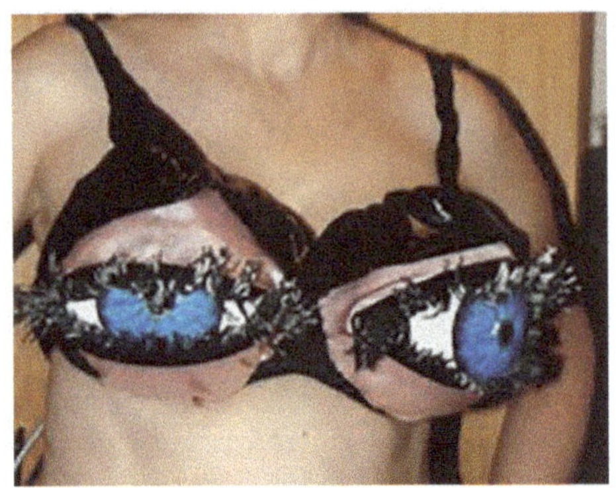

"See Cup" – this creation winks

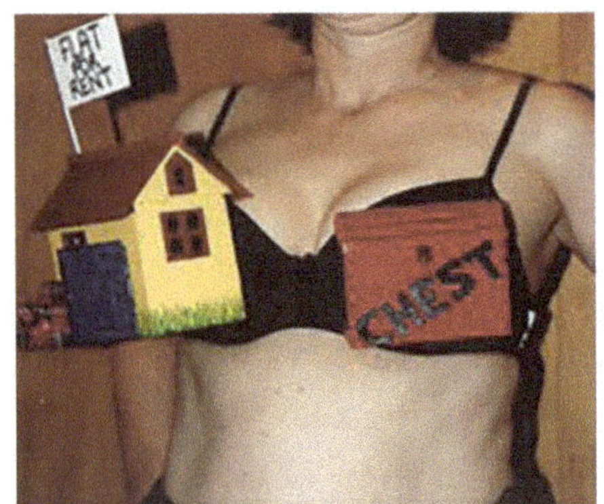

"Flat chested"

"Two Two Tutus"

Putting her WOW experience behind her, Jennie sought out other creative development opportunities. Researching what was on offer she enrolled with the Learning Connexion in Taita. "I really wanted to learn something new, so after getting a prospectus, I had a good look around the premises, including the workshops in the Hutt Valley. When I viewed the jewellery room, I was very excited at what I saw - I was like a kid in the lolly shop"! Jennie immediately signed up for all of the creative pursuits that were on offer, which included painting, photography, Oamaru stone carving, glass casting ceramics, bronze casting, and sterling silver jewellery making.   By this time Jennie was in her mid-50's but she knew, "It's never too late to learn"!

Over the next four years, Jennie went to class every Monday, Tuesday and Wednesday each week. "It was such a transition – I adored it and really found my niche". She said, "As a mature student I made so many friends. I was like a sponge and soaked up all the learning and was able to think of all kinds of things outside the box". Jennie said, "While I loved all of the classes, I fell in love with making jewellery, specifically carved and cast glass and sterling silver. Working in this craft, I could bring my vision to life and worked like a soldier to complete my projects".

Before graduating with a Diploma in Art with Honours, majoring in Jewellery, Jennie purchased a piece of equipment each month and began making jewellery from home. "I knew that life was ticking by, and I wanted to get on with it". She set up her own business from home and to this day, six years later, she has never looked back.   "The natural world continues to be my source of artistic inspiration, and I am constantly experiencing new ideas. I do a lot of sketches and collect natural material to create my designs". Jennie is particularly known for her acorn designs. She has English roots, so the acorn is meaningful to her. As she said, "The acorn signals the beginning of a new life. It took a term to perfect the glass acorn, and the top of the acorn is cast in silver". These items are very popular, and she sells a lot of them in galleries (Tennyson Gallery in Napier, Pataka in Porirua, The Dowse in Lower Hutt, Zea You Gallery in Taupo, Form Gallery in Christchurch, Soul Gallery in Hamilton, and Katie Brown's studio 'Brown & Co' in Whanganui). Information and photographs of Jennie's contemporary jewellery designs are available on her website www.jensherwin.co.nz

Jennie said, "Studying later in life truly was a life changing experience for me. Based on my personal experience I advise people to always follow their passion - follow your heart. Anything is possible. Don't listen to the naysayers. When I was younger, I would never have believed I would do this. Later in life, I realised I had so much to learn, and I just pushed myself. You have to have a dream". Jennie admits it took a lot of work to get her jewellery into the galleries, "On the one hand you use your creative streak, on the other hand it's how you run the business, and how you market your products".

The highlight of Jennie's career came when she went to Christchurch for Peter's work three years ago. The couple lived in Christchurch for 20 months, and while there Jennie joined the Silversmith Guild. "I loved it. This was my happy place. I had the skills and experience to share with others, and I met other people who would similarly share their skills and experience with me". While there she received an email from Artistar Jewels in Milan, a project by Prodes Italia Group inviting her to participate in Fashion Week - their international high-profile event. Artistar Jewels is the "reference point for all contemporary jewellery artists and designers". Jennie was invited to submit 10 pieces of her jewellery collection. "It was such an honour and a privilege to be invited to take part in this coveted event that attracts international media and guarantees high visibility in the sector". Excited by the prospect, Jennie carefully chose items from her jewellery collection and made her submission. She was thrilled when the judges accepted two of her pieces, both made in sterling silver – her Baby Acorn Earrings plated with 9 carat gold, and her Gum Leaf Nut Cluster necklace set with CZ stones.

On hearing the news Peter said, "This is such an achievement. We should all go to the opening event of the Milano Jewellery Week Exhibition in Italy". After much discussion, all of the family went to Milan for the event, including the Awards and Presentation Night. Jennie said, "I had a ball. When I saw my pieces on display, I had to pinch myself"! As one of the selected participants, Jennie's jewellery featured in the Artistar Jewels Exhibition edition, which was subsequently distributed to galleries, bookshops, and international journalists.

Although Jennie has been invited to participate in Fashion Week again, she said, "I was deeply honoured, and it was so special, but once is enough! The cost has become quite prohibitive, which doesn't even include the travel"!

Jennie is a fine example of what can happen when you follow your passion and put yourself out there in the big wide world. Now in her 60's, she works on her jewellery collection several days a week in her home studio. She is never short of inspiration for her work, does lots of sketches, designs commissioned pieces on request and gains so much satisfaction as a contemporary jeweller. "I keep a gratitude journal as I believe in the power of positive thought". As an expression of their gratitude, Jennie and Peter actively support the Philipp Family Foundation Charitable Trust.

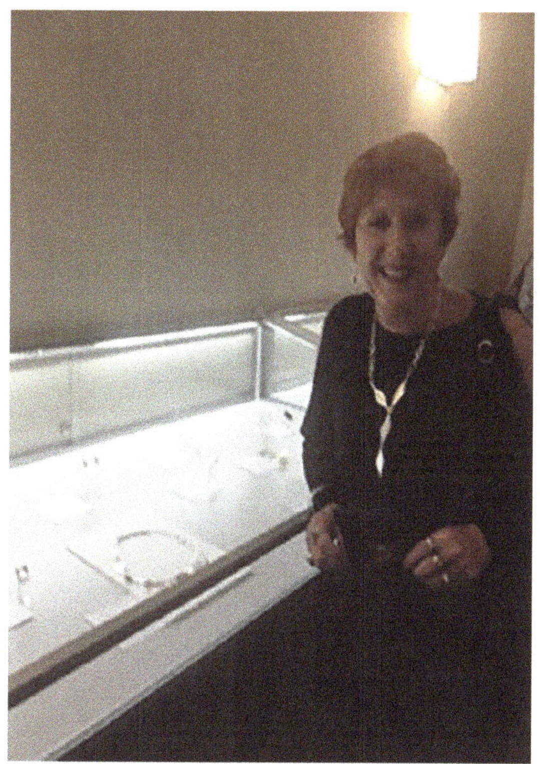

Jennie Sherwin
Photo taken at Artistar Jewels in Milan

JOHN SKENE

Approaching 70 John said, "I feel like I'm only just getting started. All of my experiences to date add up, and I'm looking forward to what's coming next"!

An only child, John was born in Irvine on the Firth of Clyde in Ayrshire, Scotland. His father was a merchant navy sailor who, from an early age, enjoyed his life at sea, but he also relished his life on shore. To John, his dad seemed to live a dual existence with long periods away from home when he was growing up. While his father was captivated by all aspects of seamanship, for as long as he can remember, John has always been enamoured with aircraft.

As a young teenager he joined the Air Training Corps and was lucky enough to visit RAF bases and experience flying in de Havilland Chipmunk aircraft. This was during the Cold War - an exciting time for an aviation enthusiast, as there were many opportunities to see the operational aircraft of the day exercising over Scottish skies. Around this time, John's father was the skipper on cargo ships belonging to ICI, carrying explosive and other cargo around the UK and ports in Europe. There was however talk of changes.

In September 1966, the family embarked on a huge adventure when they left Scotland and emigrated to New Zealand. John, then 14 years old, recalls, "It was all quite exciting. It was at the height of immigration and there were children and families relocating to the southern hemisphere from all over the world. The journey south was interesting, as we sailed through the Mediterranean Sea and down the Suez Canal to the Red Sea, then on to Australia and New Zealand. An enduring memory I have of this time was that I was too old for the children's activities and too young for the adult ones. I saw a lot of movies in the ship's cinema."

Settling in Christchurch John's father initially worked locally, and his plans to be employed on the interisland ferry between Lyttleton and Wellington did not eventuate. In later life he secured work with the Lyttleton Harbour Board where he worked until he retired.

When John finished his schooling at Linwood High School in Christchurch, he could not believe his luck when, in late 1969, he was offered a five-year engineering apprenticeship with the National Airways Corporation (NAC) in Christchurch. He said, "I thought all my birthdays had come at once"! As the job was local, John lived at home for the first three and a half years of his apprenticeship. As part of his training John spent six months working for NAC engineering at Auckland airport. "Being an only child, it was the first time I'd ever spent time away from home", he said. By the time John returned to Christchurch to finish the final year of his apprenticeship, he'd learned to enjoy his independence, so he left home to go flatting.

John really enjoyed every aspect of his apprenticeship. During this time, he also learned to fly with the Canterbury Aero Club in Piper Cherokee and Beagle Pup aircraft. Like several of his contemporaries he achieved his pilot's licence and continued to fly locally and around the South Island. Reminiscing on these days he said, "I flew for the sheer joy of it. Learning to fly also helped my appreciation of aircraft engineering"!

On completion of his apprenticeship, John was thrilled to be employed as an engineer with NAC. Between 1974-1978 he worked towards obtaining his Aircraft Maintenance Engineer Licence working on DC3, Fokker Friendship, Vickers Viscount and Boeing 737-200 aircraft.

In 1976 John married his sweetheart and the couple set up home in Christchurch. Three years later Mark, their first child, arrived followed by their daughter Cheryl, who was born in 1984. Sadly, the marriage ended shortly after Cheryl was born. It was a very difficult time for the family. As an aircraft engineer John worked a six-week rotating shift to cover the various aspects of aircraft maintenance and 'tarmac' work. He continuously updated his skills gaining overhaul categories on his licence for the various aircraft. In this business a lot of the maintenance and repairs are done during the night to ready the aircraft for the next day's flying. There was of course the daily timetable to meet.

A marriage separation is never easy – everyone in the family is impacted. Not only is it emotionally stressful, its also challenging to readjust to single life and shared custody arrangements for the children. For John, this situation was compounded when his father passed away. As an only child himself, with no extended family in New Zealand, John felt he had very little support. After the separation Mark came to stay with John, and Cheryl lived with her mum in the North Island. Apart from raising his son, work became John's focus.

Meanwhile, in 1978 the government merged the domestic NAC airline with its international counterpart into a single airline under the Air New Zealand banner. In the coming years new aircraft - Boeing 737-300, ATR and Boeing 747 aircraft were introduced, and the Fokker Friendship, DC-8 and DC-10 were withdrawn. A further restructure took place, and another round of redundancies ensued. John was one of the casualties along with a number of other aircraft engineers. It was a huge personal blow for John. His career spanning more than 20 years with the airline had ended.

When the original family home was eventually sold, John bought an older home in Christchurch, which he helped finance with his redundancy payment. As he had always been good with his hands, he began renovating the property. Seeking a new career direction he enrolled in several development courses, including a small business course. He seriously considered starting his own business, but, as luck would have it, he was offered, and gratefully accepted, a maintenance role at the Living Springs Christian Camp on the Banks Peninsula. He enjoyed the job, was able to utilize his skills, and commuted back and forth to the camp each day. The hours of work fitted well with his son Mark's school start and finish times and as a result, he and his son were able to spend more time together.

As time passed, John's son became more independent and joined the St John organisation as a cadet. Eventually Mark completed his training in hotel management.

Aircraft had always been John's passion and over the years he had updated and renewed his licences to provide coverage for the overhaul of the fleet aircraft and their engines. When John was offered a day job in the Air New Zealand engine overhaul shop at Christchurch Airport, he was absolutely over the moon. Deep down he always knew he would return to his trade. Describing this job he said, "It was the best job ever. I loved it." The job was in the workshop where all the engine parts were inspected and restored. "It was a perfect match -

apparently, I was just what they needed! The aircraft engines repaired at that time included the Rolls Royce Dart and Pratt and Whitney JT8D engines for our own fleet and for a growing customer base". As a 'Certifying Engineer', John's role was to monitor the paperwork then inspect and sign off the repairs the other aircraft engineers had completed. "For the next four years I got to know the people and their skills. We worked well together, and I had a high degree of trust in the team. It was a wonderful job".

As the saying goes, 'nothing stays the same forever'. In this case John's employment contract was changed from day-work to shift-work. The new hours did not work for John, who in the meantime had remarried. He applied for a Team Leaders role in the 'Landing gear, Wheels, and Brake Repair Shop' with Air New Zealand in Christchurch. His application was successful, but it came at a price. Although the job was day work, John discovered that this was a completely different environment to work in. In the intervening years Air New Zealand had restructured its business model and operation and had introduced the Airbus 320-200 and Boeing 777 aircraft to its fleet, but the airline was struggling, a planned buyout of Ansett - a major airline group based in Melbourne, almost brought Air New Zealand to its knees. In 2006, there was another round of redundancies, and for the second time in his life John lost his job, along with many others. It was a crushing blow and a very stressful time for everyone.

Wisely, John had constantly invested in his ongoing development over the years. When 'Quality Assurance' came into vogue, he went to night school and completed a Certificate in Quality Assurance and was encouraged by the tutor to study extramurally for a Post Graduate Diploma in Quality Assurance. Looking for work in his 50's he joined a group of job seekers. Reflecting on their transferrable skills and experience one of the facilitators – an ex-NAC Air Hostess said, "I'll help you find a good job", and she did! Parkland Products Ltd imported, supplied and maintained a wide range of products for the golfing industry, and they were looking for an engineer. John applied and got the job. Recognising and acknowledging his skills, he was quickly promoted to 'Workshop Supervisor'. John worked for Parkland Products for 18 months, but sadly during this period his second marriage came to an end.

Around this time (2008) an Airworthiness Inspector's role with the Civil Aviation Authority (CAA) came to John's attention. At the time CAA was located in Petone. "I'd lived in Christchurch for most of my life. It would be a change of scenery and a change of direction, so I applied for the role and got the job", he said. John relocated to Wellington and later built a house in Carterton where he joined the local Rotary Club and got involved with the community.

He really enjoyed his new job, which was to visit and audit aircraft engineers maintaining general aviation aircraft and helicopters. This group of around 40 engineers worked under the CAA Rule Part 43 and were spread throughout the country. "These visits occurred on an annual basis. The role kept me quite busy," said John. Through this job he developed friendships with colleagues that he still maintains to this day. In 2014 John met his partner Alison and they have been together ever since.

By the time the CAA relocated its office to Wellington, John was eligible for New Zealand Superannuation. Rather than retire, he chose to continue to work for the CAA for a further 18 months on a contract basis, looking after the 'Review of Airworthiness process' (the aircraft equivalent of a warrant of fitness). During this time, he gradually reduced his hours of work from three-to-two days per week. In semi-retirement John set up a business; 'Ardrossan Holdings Ltd', which enabled him to be self-employed undertaking auditing and other contract work.

In 2018, John and Alison relocated to Waikanae. It was a good decision - "We really like the climate and the atmosphere on the Kāpiti Coast, and are very happy here", he said. Now John is very involved with the local MenzShed and belongs to the Entrepreneurs at 50+ Network. He also initiated a monthly network/coffee catch up for aviation friends and enthusiasts, "We all come from different backgrounds with different experiences. Some are pilots, some are engineers. There's a real mix of personalities and we all share a passion for aviation."

Over more than six decades John has accumulated a large collection of aviation books and memorabilia. Given his passion, research, and practical experience, he has become an authority on a wide range of aircraft, their engines and the people associated with them. John shares his aviation knowledge and stories with the community in his monthly radio programme called "Aviation Past and Present" (for more information see Aviation, Past and Present (coastaccesradio.org.nz). Looking to the future he plans to publish a collection of stories about aircraft and the people connected with them. As a budding aviation historian, he also assists others to research and

Creating Life On Our Own Terms document

their aviation experience/stories.

"Aviation in itself is not inherently dangerous. But to an even greater degree than the sea, it is terribly unforgiving of any carelessness, incapacity or neglect."

Captain A. G. Lamplugh, British Aviation Insurance Group, London. 1930's

Young John on the wreck of a Spartan Cruiser 3
Hill of Stake, Muirshiel Park (West of Glasgow)

John at the WW1 Aviation Display, Omaka Heritage Centre, Blenheim

John in a two-seater glider at Papawai Airfield, Greytown

John with a Hawker Harrier GR3 vertical take-off fighter
Ashburton Aviation Museum

GAYLENE DENFORD-WOOD

Gaylene, the oldest of four in her family, grew up on the Taieri (meaning fertile plain), southwest of Dunedin. Her paternal great, great grandparents John and Mary Thomson had sailed from Dumfries, Scotland into Otago Harbour aboard the *Cheviot*, in 1862. Farmers, they built their home, *'The Banks'* on the foothills of Maungatua. Growing up in this rural community Gaylene said, "I had a wonderful childhood, full of adventure." Elaborating she said, "These were the days when the boundaries were clear. Once our share of the chores was done, we were free to go off for the rest of the day on our bikes, alone or with friends, as long as we were back for dinner or before dark". Casting her mind back Gaylene vividly recalls climbing to the top of Maungatua by herself when she was only nine years old. "The air was alive with the song of skylarks, and I knew of the presence up there of rare orchids. When I reached the top, I could see the sea! It was a defining moment for me.

A sketch of Maungatua Gaylene made as a child

So enthusiastic was I on returning home, I was charged with leading a small party back up to the summit the following weekend – this time, recording highlights with my *Box Brownie* for which I'd saved my sixpence-a-week pocket money over many months."

Gaylene enjoyed her schooldays at Outram Primary School and was Head Girl in her final year. "I knew from an early age that I wanted to be a teacher, inspired, in turn, by my teachers, Ida Robertson, Alexander Peter Allen, and Stanley James". She turned down the chance to be a boarder at Timaru Girls, instead attending The Taieri High School where she was a prefect in her senior two years and left with University Entrance accredited. During this time the old Taieri Aerodrome was replaced in 1962 by the new Dunedin Airport at Momona, several farms' lengths down the road from *'Glen Isla'* that her parents had pioneered into a successful dairy farm. There in the summer holidays she swapped hay making for hospitality. Employed by the new *Skychef* restaurant, she served travellers from all over the world.

Gaylene in her first job at the Airport

In 1967, as an independent young woman looking forward to

making her own way in the world, she left home to study at the University of Canterbury in Christchurch. Initially, she studied Fine Arts, deeply influenced by the work of Bill Sutton, Doris Lusk, and Don Peebles, among others who were, in her view, exemplary tutors as was later, the painter, John Coley. The history of art though, she valued most of all for the way in which it mirrored the evolution of human consciousness. Part way through her studies Gaylene remembers pacing alongside the willow lined Avon River, over-analytically asking herself, "Do I really want to specialise? I saw a stick buoyed along by the current and watched how it touched in turn, the right bank then the left, and took it as a metaphor for following both my heart and my mind", which is what she did! Gaylene traded one bursary for another to go to Christchurch Teachers' College where she applied for the new three-year programme. Following a memorable interview with principals, Jean Herbison and Dr Jack Mann at a long table in the Gothic Revival building (known pre-earthquake as *The Peterborough*), she was encouraged and reassured that she had made the right decision when they said, "We need mature students like you who know where they are going"!

Graduating from Teachers' College in 1970, and having earlier that year, married Michael her childhood sweetheart, a civil engineer with the Ministry of Works, the newly-weds set up home in Christchurch, where they began to establish their professional careers and where their two children Philip and Antonia were born. In their spare time as members of the Canterbury University Car Club, they enjoyed car trialling in their Volkswagen (VW), which involved team coordination of driving, navigating and timekeeping and was "lots of fun". Gaylene won several prizes for navigation and a table lamp for her night driving on the loose gravel roads of Canterbury's hinterland. Weekends saw them 'yumping' (adventure sports) in their VW, fording rivers as well as South Island adventures when they drove over the Old Man and Old Woman Ranges (Kopuwai Ranges in Central Otago), for the sheer challenge and adventure of it. When their first child was born, Gaylene became a stay-at-home Mum, while Michael studied for his PhD in hydrology with the support of his future employer.

In 1973 following her husband's graduation, he was transferred to head office in the Systems Laboratory, Wellington. Gaylene said, "We boarded the ferry in Lyttelton, and woke up the next morning docked at Queens Wharf" – that's how it was in those days. They were allocated one of the Ministry of Works houses in Mary Huse Grove, Manor Park where "the occupants were engineers on transfer, mostly men married to teachers or nurses and with young children of a similar age. It was very homogeneous compared with the university culture we were accustomed to." The playcentre and school were central to this community of young families starting out in life, Gaylene recalls, "It was a mini-society in one street, ethically, environmentally and community oriented". Families supported one another, "particularly the mothers who provided a casual network of home-based quality childcare, supporting one another to re-enter the workforce part time, to upskill and re-find wider confidence in the wake of fulltime motherhood".

Residents socialised together, held whole street progressive dinners, and invited speakers to come and talk to them. Gaylene recalls that it was at one of these dinners in August 1974, when they heard that the popular Prime Minister, Norman Kirk, had suddenly died. Gaylene said, "the party was stunned into silence by the news". Following Norman Kirk's untimely death, tens of thousands of people filed past his coffin when it lay in state in Parliament House in Wellington. The population went into mourning and memorial services were held all around New Zealand.

The 1970's was a time of societal change in New Zealand. Families were keen to buy their own homes. The feminist movement was gaining momentum (Gaylene was involved with the first United Women's Convention held in Wellington) and gender stereotyping was challenged. Views on shared parenting became more prevalent. Gaylene recalls that Manor Park Playcentre was one of the first to have a high proportion of father-helpers at its sessions, and more and more women looked to return to the workforce when their children started school. By this time Gaylene's oldest child was at school, and she and her husband were looking to buy a home of their own. Gaylene took up a part-time market research job, "in order to explore the suburbs on foot to get a feel, firsthand, of where in Wellington, it would be apt to house-hunt". The market research soon led to a fork in the road. One path saw her conducting a fossil fuel investigation in the South Island from which her findings led to being flown to Auckland to meet with the company directors. She enjoyed this challenging assignment immensely. Equally, her leadership roles in the Playcentre movement led to several early childhood research projects, one of which was as a research assistant for New Zealand Council for Educational Research (NZCER). Gaylene said she will never forget as a twenty-something-year-old Playcentre mother, being introduced to research methods by Dr Geraldine McDonald whose knowledge had her eager, on the edge of her seat! Subsequently she was offered a fulltime market research role, heading a feasibility study for a Turoa ski-field. Although tempting, her daughter was six months short of her fifth birthday. It was a water-shed moment. She knew that however interesting this path may prove to be, her true calling and preferred service was to education and research in that field.

Gaylene also helped set up support groups for children, who for one reason or another were separated from their primary caregivers through hospitalisation, imprisonment, and unregulated forms of childcare. This work followed the visit to New Zealand of the Robertsons from the Tavistock Institute, a not-for-profit organisation that applies social science to contemporary issues and problems.

Getting on with life, time passed quickly. The children were growing up, but unfortunately the couple had grown apart. After 17 years of marriage Gaylene and her husband amicably decided to go their separate ways. However, they remain on good terms which "feels like a blessing at extended family gatherings".

Gaylene continued in her early childhood leadership roles whilst teaching at Parkway Intermediate and at Pencarrow School. Specialising in accelerated maths and reading recovery, she received a call to join the college of teachers in the pioneering of a new Steiner school, initially for children aged four years to Year 8. It was at the 1979 Early Childhood Care & Development Convention at the University of Canterbury, after Marie Bell from the Education Department had asked her to lead an introductory workshop, that Gaylene was coincidentally introduced to the growing interest in this form of education. Its focus on integrated learning and the quality of student work had caught her attention. Prompted by her Playcentre friend and colleague, Tessa Hope-Williams, she had been looking carefully into it. Thus, later, through professional connections, Gaylene met Paul who shared her love of teaching and learning. The relationship blossomed into marriage and their respective families expanded with the arrival of their son John-Paul in 1993 (when Gaylene was 45). Now they had four children between them.

Around this time Gaylene was facilitating Ministry funded teacher education courses and implementing various teaching and learning methodologies to get the best outcomes for the students. She was also a regular guest lecturer at Victoria University of Wellington where her research focus was valued. When one of the senior lecturers suggested she should consider doing a master's degree and offered to supervise her thesis, Gaylene enrolled and subsequently began an academic career path. Whilst completing her thesis, 'Becoming and Being an Effective Steiner Teacher', she was asked to help set up a degree course at Auckland University of Technology (AUT). At the time the family were living in the Wairarapa, so Gaylene commuted backwards and forwards to Auckland each week. The fruits of her work were so successful that within a year, through the academic promotions round, she was appointed as a Senior Lecturer. This was a role she cherished as the work comprised a blend of research and teaching, which gave her so much joy, and she saw how often student learning was transformative. Some students even wrote to her years later, to say how much the course had meant to them.

In 2012 Gaylene flew to Paris, took the train south to St Jean Pied de Port and walked the Camino Santiago de Compostela, a pilgrimage trail across northern Spain that attracts people from all over the world. An opportunity to step away from the day-to-day busyness of life, "the walk allows the time and space to reconnect with ourselves, with something greater than ourselves, with others and with nature". The process of simply walking through ever-changing landscape enables us to "slow down, recognise the essential, and embrace simplicity". This was something Gaylene had not contemplated doing but suddenly, through a chance conversation with friends, it presented itself as a next vital step! What's more, in her 60's, she chose to do this trip by herself. Following in the footsteps of medieval pilgrims, the original *Camino Frances,* or French Way, "crosses the Pyrenees into undulating fields and olive groves, vineyards and landscape dotted with oak forest, through mountains, river valleys and cities". After climbing to the high plateau of the Meseta and on through the greenness of Galicia, the path finally takes a sweeping descent into the cathedral city of Santiago (Saint James). (This reminded Gaylene that, according to her parents, she had taken her very first step when learning to walk into the arms of her Grandfather James from *The Banks*.) Gaylene clocked up over 830 kilometres in 29 days and met many interesting people of different nationalities and walks of life. Through conversation involving deep listening, she found that most of them "were working through life issues such as grief, work related problems and stuck relationships". Recalling the experience Gaylene said, "I felt so privileged to do this walk unencumbered, to feel so happy, healthy, and blister-free. The very rhythmical nature of walking itself is life engendering". Her guidebook encouraged "walking with consciousness" - creating a deeper level of awareness in the present and connecting with everything around. Gaylene, who had practiced meditation for decades, found the Camino experience both exhilarating and profound. By the final day of the walk, just short of a month, she had connected with her inner voice, from which came the metaphor for her next thesis – this for Gaylene, was another defining moment.

The following year Gaylene was introduced to a poetic form that, as her thesis outlines, "when used mindfully, can foster vitality, self-realisation and meaningfulness". Captivated by the notion of socio-poetic mindfulness for teachers, the more she investigated the concept and the possibilities that this poetic form, used as a practice, might have on wellbeing, the more she was drawn to undertake in-depth research in this area. Gaylene had discovered a compelling topic for her PhD. The biggest and most crucial challenge was to identify the right Supervisors who not only shared her interest in her research topic, and willing to share their expertise, but were also willing to collaborate with her throughout her learning journey. After a couple of false starts Gaylene finally met the right person – Dr Leigh Burrows at Flinders University in Australia. Leigh was the first person she had met who very quickly grasped and supported what she was trying to do. Leigh identified with the "originality and potential" of her research and offered to be her Principal Supervisor. It was a perfect match. Soon Associate Professor Kathy Arthurson, whom Gaylene met when they presented together at a conference in Wollongong, became her Associate Supervisor. Gaylene's PhD research proposal was endorsed at Flinders University in 2015.

Three years later, "after much concentrated work with amazing co-researchers based in Aotearoa and in the UK", Gaylene graduated with her doctorate at 70 years of age. Seminaria is the name she gave to the poetic form. Her thesis explains what people discovered from using it as a daily mindfulness practice. Following her graduation in 2018 came a further moment of recognition in May 2019 when Gaylene was awarded the Vice-Chancellor's prize for Academic Excellence for her thesis, '*The mindfulness of seminaria': A heuristic inquiry with teachers and leaders uncovers a poetry path to wellbeing.* For Gaylene "it was a great honour" and a tremendous achievement! One of the joys for her is seeing how the value of her evidence-based research is spreading beyond the framework of education, to find wider application and service in the social sciences.

As a result of her transformational learning experience Gaylene approaches her life and her work with renewed energy and enthusiasm. Following her graduation, she set up 'The Mindfulness of Seminaria', to teach others how to use the poetic form "to distil and discover the essence of any matter and help realise their own potential for self-mastery". Through her professional practice she offers creative workshops for the community. She has also been invited to hold workshops for professional groups such as health care workers, celebrants, the Samoan Community, teachers, and educational leaders. Some are now using her work in hospice care as well as in correctional and detention facilities. In her workshops, Gaylene introduces the mindfulness of seminaria in novel ways facilitating "the writing of poetry as a new way of seeing". Her innovative research has generated widespread national and international interest in academic journals. With growing interest in her work, she is often invited to speak at conferences. Check out Gaylene's website www.themindfulnessofseminaria.co.nz to learn more about her research, access her publications, presentations, and find out more about her upcoming workshops.

Gaylene and her husband Paul currently reside in Korokoro near Wellington. For them, chronological age is of little consequence. Pursuing their love of learning, and an ethos of service, they lead happy and fulfilling lives, and enjoy spending quality time with their four adult children and three grandchildren.

'Yumping' in the mountains of Central Otago

Artist Heather Grouden helps Gaylene halve her sculpture to fit the kiln

Being fitted in doctoral regalia   Gaylene Denford-Wood

Gaylene with daughter Antonia, son-in-law Steve and their children

KEVIN BOYCE

Growing up in Christchurch, Kevin, the second eldest of four children, wanted to be a Vet. He enjoyed school and motivated to complete his final year at Papanui High School, he earned his keep by delivering groceries after school during the week and milk on the weekends. His favourite subjects were History, Mathematics, Music and Sport. In his final year at Papanui High, he was an appointed Prefect, Captain of the First 11 Hockey Team, a member of the Tennis 8. He was the baritone player in the school's Brass Band and, with a low range singing voice, was a baritone in the school's choirs and musicals. He recalls it came as a bit of a surprise to learn that in addition to Mathematics, he should have studied Biology, Chemistry and Physics, in his last year at school, in order to qualify for a veterinary science degree! Thankfully a Career Advisor recognised Kevin's potential and suggested he train as a teacher. Taking the advice, Kevin applied and was accepted at Christchurch Teachers' Training College. This was a defining moment, as this year Kevin celebrates a significant milestone in his career: 50 years in Education, 34 of these years in private schools, and 30 of these years as a principal. His four Principalships were in leading schools, with a Christian ethos in alignment with his strong faith.

Kevin began his teachers' training course, in 1967: the year that New Zealand dispensed with pounds, shillings and pence and adopted decimal currency. The transition to 'earning while learning' was very exciting, as in those days' student teachers were paid $8 a week for the duration of their training. Kevin lived at home while he studied, "It came as a bit of a shock that

I had to pay my Mum $3 a week board!" His mother did say that his board would be $3 forever and Kevin was tempted to return years later and say, "I'm back and expecting no inflation in my boarding charges!" At Teachers College he was particularly inspired by Dame Jean Herbison, the Deputy Principal, "within three days she knew every student by name. A great role model she showed us that every student mattered." Dame Jean's philosophy resonated with him and 'Every child counts no-one left behind' was promoted by Kevin throughout his career. Dame Jean became a mentor for Kevin and his fellow students, including Dave Wootton. More than three decades later, Kevin met Dame Jean again at David's funeral, and "despite the passage of time, she remembered me and my name!"

Kevin loved his time at teachers' training college. During these years he taught himself how to play folk guitar, and later learned finger style and classical guitar in a 'Music Selected' study course. He was also heavily involved in drama, folk singing groups and madrigal singing, especially musicals. In his final year, he specialised in Music and Maths: "a great combination for future teaching". He entered the nationwide 'Mobil Singing Contest' and, as a member of the jug band 'Uncle Reuben's Goodtime Boys', performed a number of original numbers at College events.

In 1970, following his graduation, Kevin began his teaching career in the public school system in Christchurch. For the first three years he taught in Canterbury at Cotswold Primary School before securing a position at Glenmoor Primary. In 1972, quite by chance, Kevin heard they were looking for a teacher in his area of specialisation at Hadlow, a private preparatory school in Masterton (now part of the Trinity Schools). When he applied for the role, he was very impressed with the interview and selection process, and was bowled over when he was offered his dream job "all done, on trust, by the headmaster and the job 'signed and sealed' on a handshake"!

At Hadlow there was a strong sense of belonging and respect amongst the staff and the students, and Kevin's areas of specialisation and expertise were embraced within the community. During the three years Kevin taught at Hadlow, he coached the cricket, hockey, rugby, and soccer teams. A highlight, during his tenure, was organising and producing 'Joseph and the Amazing Technicolour Dreamcoat', one of the world's most popular musicals. Kevin credits his Teachers' College best mate Conal Atkins, for this major undertaking, as he'd seen the show in London and had returned to Hadlow to teach. During the practices, Kevin dislocated his right shoulder and had to conduct the 90 strong choir and orchestra with his left arm. Director Atkins quipped, "it was great working with a "one armed conductor, who could well be sought after later as a paper hanger!" The performances were a huge success with the Hadlow community, and to this day, this production is fondly remembered. The two Hadlow staff that influenced Kevin's educational direction were Ian Harper, who mentored male staff-members as they pursued their vision of realising a Preparatory School Headship, and Ivon Aitkenhead, twice an All Black trialist, who was a ready listener and motivator.

As time passed, Kevin resigned from his role and moved to London for 1976 and 1977 to gain some overseas teaching experience. In the UK, he taught at Shirley High School in Croydon. "I played league hockey for the Old Mid-Whitgiftian's, the 'Old Boys' team of the Trinity Schools of John Whitgift, who, as the Archbishop of Canterbury was at the bedside of Queen Elizabeth 1st as she died in 1603"! He also taught at St John's Church School, where once again he facilitated a production of 'Joseph and the Amazing Technicolour Dreamcoat'. Kevin said, "the standard of Music at St John's was second to none, boasting sons of the Kings' and Mike Sammes' Singers on their roll". Here Kevin coached the school's football team, which won the London Small Schools' Cup in 1977, "the soccer skill, of these young boys, was inherent and every day they built on their talents at morning intervals and lunch breaks". Three highlights, in London, were being an official at the UK Athletics' trials for the 1976 Olympics, seeing his boyhood hero George Best play for Fulham against Crystal Palace, and stopping a schoolboy football match, so that he could observe Concorde flying overhead "much to the consternation of the opposition coach!"

In those days New Zealand (NZ) teachers had to re-train if their stay overseas exceeded three years. Returning home within the time-frame, Kevin secured a teaching position at Mangatoki School, a three-teacher school, near Eltham, in Taranaki. He recalls, "We rented a house for $6 a week, from a kindly person in the community. While we were there, our first child Ben was born in the Stratford Maternity Annex." Within 12 months, Alan Cooper, the newly appointed Headmaster at Hadlow invited Kevin to run the Boarding House and be Deputy Headmaster. With Alan at the helm, Hadlow's school roll had expanded, and their teaching staff had increased from five to eight. Although sorry to leave Taranaki, this fantastic opportunity was too good to miss. Kevin, aged 29, accepted the invitation, and with that, his career went from strength to strength.

Under Alan's leadership, the team at Hadlow developed the school's reputation and grew the student numbers. When Alan resigned from the role, in 1982, to become the Principal of St George's School in Whanganui, Kevin was sorry to see him go. As the saying goes, 'when one door closes another door opens' - this was the case for Kevin, who at 33 years of age, with Alan's support, applied for and was appointed as the Headmaster of Hadlow Preparatory School. In the coming years the school roll expanded with more than 200 students. The Boarding House had 65 boarders (56 boys and nine girls, including four orphans). In 1983 a pre-school was started by Kevin. His son Ben, and daughter, Amelia, born in 1982, were both pupils at Hadlow's Pre-School. Every year Hadlow put on a major musical production, which included, 'The Wizard of Oz', 'Tom Sawyer', 'Joseph and the Amazing Technicolour Dreamcoat', and 'Oliver'. Kevin is full of pride for the students and the staff, who participated in these impressive events for the community. He recalls all of Masterton's primary schools, came to watch 'Oliver'.

Whilst in the Wairarapa, Kevin trained as a Contract Announcer for Radio 2ZD reporting on local sport. Highlights were forming a lifetime friendship with Sir Brian Lochore, seeing the elder rugby statesman, George Nepia, watching his grandson, Bill Rowlands, who was to prop against four Lions' teams, playing a Senior rugby game – a game Kevin reported on for Radio Wairarapa. Another highlight for Kevin, was when Princess Diana visited NZ in 1983. He had the opportunity to meet her at Queen Elizabeth Park, where all of the local Schools were invited to get a glimpse of this beautiful royal. After walking and talking to the Hadlow School pupils, Princess Diana stopped in front of Kevin and asked, "Are you the headmaster?" Kevin replied, "Yes M'me", to which Diana asked, "Are these all your children?". "Not mine personally M'me" he responded. Kevin recalls Princess Diana quickly quipped, "I thought that there was family planning in NZ!"

A young Headmaster, Kevin Boyce, meets Princess Diana in 1983

The NZ Preparatory Schools' scene had a hierarchy within their system, in terms of Sports' exchanges and results. The 3H's: Hadlow, Hereworth and Huntley, endorsed this close rivalry. The prime example was the sporting prowess of Huntley Prep School, in Marton, that boasted no home losses, by their Ist XV rugby team, in 13 years. In the Hadlow v Huntley rivalry, Hadlow had not scored a Ist XV win in 16 years of competition. The Hadlow Ist XV of 1985, coached by George Mahupuku, who had Captained the Maori All Blacks, and a Huntley Old Boy, Neil McWhannell, who had inside knowledge of the Huntley match preparation rituals, broke Huntley's proud record. The Wairarapa Times' Age called Hadlow's 13-12 victory a 'trouncing' (Masterton had waited a long time for this win!). Kevin said, "Hadlow has produced several National/

International representatives, including Albert Hawea, NZ Secondary Schools Rugby, Malcolm Holmes, NZ Secondary Schools' Rugby Captain, and Marcus Daniell, Tennis".

In 1988, in recognition of Kevin's service to the Trinity Schools, he was granted a term's educational research sabbatical in Australia. The Boyce family based themselves in Melbourne, where Amelia and Ben attended Balwyn North school, while Kevin completed his research project. Kevin said, "It was a fabulous development opportunity. I visited 25 schools in six states and the two mainland territories in Australia, including a visit to the Flying Doctor school in Alice Springs." He subsequently presented his research report to the Trinity Schools' community and his colleagues in the NZ Private Schools' system, later to be called 'Independent Schools of NZ'.

Returning to NZ the family moved back into their home and Kevin went back to Hadlow, but after 19 years of marriage, Kevin and his wife Jenny parted ways. It was a very difficult time for the whole family, who were an integral part of the community, and there was a period of adjustment. Five of Kevin's eight staff members were later to become school Principals, fulfilling Kevin's philosophy of developing staff for the next promotional step in their careers. After seven years as Headmaster at Hadlow, Kevin resigned and relocated to Wellington to work in a corporate role.

As an Accounts' Executive for Marketing Impact, Kevin worked on multiple projects. He enjoyed his new job but, given the physical distance between Masterton and Wellington (a two-hour commute each way), the agreed shared custody arrangement was challenging to manage, and Kevin and his children missed spending time together on a day-to-day basis.

When offered the Acting Head Teacher role at Chanel College, Kevin gratefully accepted the job and shifted back to the Wairarapa to be closer to his children. Within a year he was offered the Year 9 Dean's role at Chanel College. Over the next three years he created A-Stream classes in Years 9 and 10, and taught School Certificate English and History. He also facilitated and performed in several successful major productions, including the black comedy musical, 'Little Shop of Horrors', 'The Pyjama Game', 'Who Dunnit', and 'Theatre Sports' (winning the inaugural Wairarapa title with a group of local thespians).

Kevin met his second wife, Dianne on a blind date, subsequently winning a couples' competition, at Solway Park, on their first outing together! Dianne also had two children (James and Kate). The relationship flourished and they married in 1994. When he was appointed Head of the Preparatory School, at Scots College, in Wellington, the couple resided in Paraparaumu before setting up home in the eastern suburb of Seatoun. The Boyce family expanded when their daughter Bekky was born three years later.

As with his previous roles, Kevin maintained strong numbers at Scots. He took great delight in the Preparatory boys' achievements academically, culturally, socially, and spiritually. Physical education and sport were key parts of the curriculum. Boys of all ages were encouraged to participate in a variety of sports and learn how to work and play together as a team. With these dynamics and, those of performing to the best of one's ability, were skills that could be transferred into a classroom setting. During Kevin's seven years at the helm of the Scots' Preparatory School, Scholarships were gained by boys at Kings

College, Rathkeale, Scots' Secondary, and Whanganui Collegiate. Kevin's philosophy, "that each student realises his potential" was always paramount. He encouraged the Preparatory School to present regular productions, including 'Be-Bop a Lula', 'Blast Off', 'Bugsy Malone', and 'The Pied Piper'. The Preparatory School's choir was also invited twice to sing with the NZ Symphony Orchestra.

Kevin coached team sports, and organised and led the school's Ist Rugby, Hockey and Soccer teams on a trip to Australia to compete with their Independent Schools' counterparts. Naturally, any child who gets an opportunity like this is over the moon. Kevin recalls one of the students was Victor Vito, who had been given a Scholarship to Scots' Preparatory School as an 8-year-old, already boasting a size 9 shoe! This talented youngster played in the school's 1st XV. Victor became a well-known NZ rugby player, playing for the NZ Secondary School team, NZ Sevens, the Hurricanes and later 33 games for the All Blacks. Victor now plays with a French rugby union club. On reflection Kevin said, "We are told that teachers make differences to every child's life. Whilst it's not an easy role, it is rewarding to know you have contributed to another's success in life and part of something much bigger than you can ever imagine". Some years later, after Victor's successes, Kevin was 'blown away' to receive a four-page handwritten letter from Victor saying 'thank you' for the opportunities that he received by being given a place at Scots, and how this had stood him in good stead for his future as a professional rugby player, now with a size 16 shoe!

Whilst at Scots, the College hosted the Presbyterian Quadrangular (Lindisfarne, St. Andrews, St Kentigern and Scots) annual rugby tournament. Ian McKinnon had booked the Grand Hall of Parliament for the tournament dinner. Kevin asked B.J. Lochore to be the guest speaker. At the conclusion of Sir Brian's speech to these young men, he said, "Your parents have poured a lot of time and money into your college careers. Have you ever thanked them? Just before Christmas find a time to shake the hands of Mum and Dad and say thank you!" Kevin said, "You could imagine many startled parents being approached and asking, 'who told you to do this?'"

After seven years' service, Kevin resigned from his role at Scots to become the Principal of St Michaels School, in the centre of Christchurch. Founded in 1851, this Anglican Church School, the oldest in the Canterbury region, has a long-standing tradition of choral music, drama, and the arts. The school's heritage appealed to Kevin, and he was returning to his hometown, where his teaching career had begun more than 30 years earlier. At the time, the school had 161 students with a falling roll, and the buildings needed refurbishing. Kevin loves a challenge and couldn't wait to get started.

The impetus for the major renovation project was St Michael's sesqui-centenary celebrations in 2001. Working in partnership with the School Trustees and the local community, plans were drawn up, and three-million-dollar funding targets were set and raised to restore and modernise the school's buildings and facilities. At the same time, a great deal of work went into planning and organising St Michael's 150th year celebrations, which were well attended and a huge success. A true strength was St. Michael's multi-cultural roll, with one Chinese family proud of five generations following each other to 'their' School. Meanwhile, the school continued to function, and all of the additional activity put St Michael's back on the map. Within five years the school roll had increased by 25%. Biennial productions were reintroduced. These were so popular, that the school had to present these offsite in local Secondary Halls and also in the Majestic Theatre, where the Beatles had performed in 1964!

The years passed, everything was going well, when disaster struck on 4 September 2010. At 4.35am, an earthquake, with a magnitude of 7.1, shook the city of Christchurch. It was a terrifying experience. Kevin recalls, "I thought our modern townhouse was about to do a structural somersault"! Luckily, as the quake occurred early in the morning, most people were in bed. There was no loss of life, but several were severely injured, and there was considerable damage. In the months that followed, there were thousands of smaller aftershocks, which was very unnerving for people living in the region. During this period, the school carried out regular earthquake drills with the children and emergency plans were updated. As the earthquakes registered above 5 on the Richter scale, all schools had to close until they had been checked by structural engineers. Kevin recalls, "The Board Chairman, David Irvine, provided a great source of counsel, governance knowledge, and support during these testing times".

After the summer holidays, the children returned to school in early February 2011. On Tuesday 22 February, in the middle of the day (12.51pm), a severe earthquake (magnitude of 6.3), struck the region. 'Because this aftershock was centred very close to Christchurch, it was much more destructive'. Buildings collapsed, roads and bridges were destroyed, and liquefaction and surface flooding hampered the rescue operation. There was widespread damage, particularly in the central city where St Michael's is located. Pandemonium ensued across the region as people desperately tried to reconnect with their loved ones. Amidst the chaos, the school's emergency plan was immediately implemented. The children, terrified by the experience, were comforted by the staff and kept within the school grounds until they could be released to a family member.

Although none of the children were killed, or seriously injured at St Michael's, there were 185 fatalities in the region, and thousands of people were injured. Dianne, who was Manager of Volunteers at the Cancer Society, assisted in the evacuation of work colleagues before picking up Bekky from Rangi Ruru College, and then they both waited nervously for Kevin to return. After seeing all of his students safely into the hands of their parents, Kevin 'navigated' his way home about 7pm, with his 'two ladies' pleased to see him in one piece! The family later learned that Gillie, the fiancée of Kevin's nephew, was one of the 115 people, who died in the CTV building; a double tragedy as Gillie was pregnant!

Life in the Canterbury region dramatically changed. A national state of Civil Defence Emergency was declared, and search and rescue efforts were coordinated. Power and water supply was affected and many people either had no homes to go to, or homes were badly damaged. Temporary living arrangements had to be set up. The central city was the worst affected. Labelled the 'Red Zone', it was closed to the public. Some workplaces, shops and hotels and restaurants either no longer existed, or were so badly damaged they had to be demolished. Many of the heritage buildings were damaged or destroyed.

Most of the schools in Christchurch were closed for weeks, and the staff, who also lived and worked in the same community, had their own family circumstances and sense of loss to contend with as well.

Kevin was the first person allowed inside St Michael's after the quakes and was taken aback with the $2 million damage to their 'showpiece school'. "It would take nearly ten years for the full extent of the school buildings to be reopened", he said. Kevin strongly felt the pupils, still located in Christchurch, "would find comfort in returning to a familiar setting with their classmates and teachers". He worked with the local Ministry of Education, to ensure St Michael's was one of the first schools to be up and running again. Portaloos had to be installed and access to fresh running water provided before the school could re-open. Such was the lot of a Principal - Kevin's Sunday task was to empty the schools' portable toilets! In the months that followed, there were hundreds of aftershocks - some were severe. The constant tremors felt day and night were disconcerting. Kevin spent days on the phone contacting all of his parent community, only to find, that grieving and discouraged, many left Christchurch to rebuild their lives elsewhere. The roll at St Michael's shrank to half the number they'd had before the disaster.

By the end of the 2012 school year, Kevin was exhausted and looked forward to the summer holiday. He'd really enjoyed his 13 years as the Principal at St Michaels and was proud of what had been achieved, but the impact of the earthquakes had taken its toll. Thinking it was time for a change, he took leave from St Michael's and accepted a one-year contract, with Cognition NZ, as a 'Principals' Advisor' for the ten schools on the Republic of Nauru. By this time his eldest children, Amelia and Ben were married, and their youngest daughter Bekky was in her final two years at High School. Dianne was really enjoying her job Managing 600+ volunteers for the Cancer Society, so the couple agreed that he would work in Nauru and Dianne would remain in Christchurch with Bekky for the term of the contract.

The arrangement worked well. Kevin thoroughly enjoyed life in Nauru, the third smallest country in the world, comprising eight square miles and surrounded by a coral reef. Taking the time to become familiar with the customs and practices in the towns and villages, he developed rapport with people from all walks of life, including asylum seekers, who had sought refuge on the island.   Enchanted with the people, he found the role rewarding, led the singing every Sunday at a local Church, and was invited to preach!

When his contract was extended for a further year, Kevin resigned from his job at St Michael's and promised to return to home for Bekky's Year 13 Prizegiving and School Ball. Unfortunately, while working in the 48C degree heat in Nauru, he contracted Dengue Fever and became very ill. As treatment wasn't available on the island, he was flown to Brisbane in Australia, where he was hospitalised on arrival. It was a very frightening experience. Following several weeks convalescing, Kevin returned to Nauru to complete his contract and was thrilled to sing and play in a band with the blind Nauruan organist, Samvic Namaduk. Together they recorded one of Kevin's originals, 'Christmas Day Truce', which was entered in a local competition and played on the local radio.

Returning to Christchurch, Kevin accepted the Assistant

Principal's role at Avondale Primary School, a central city school situated in the 'Red Zone' (the area that experienced severe damage in the disaster following the Christchurch earthquakes). At the time, Avondale's future was uncertain, along with several other schools that had been damaged. Eventually, the school was one of four that closed in 2017 to make way for a new super-school that was built in the city. In the aftermath of the earthquakes, Christchurch changed. Whilst the community spirit was strong, day to day life was challenging. Many families with children moved away to start afresh elsewhere and consequently school rolls shrank even further. By this time Bekky had left school and Dianne and Kevin made the decision to begin the next chapter of their lives in the North Island.

Relocating to the Kāpiti Coast, the couple bought a house in Raumati Beach, with fantastic views of both Kāpiti Island and the Tararua Ranges. For the next three years Kevin commuted to his job in Wellington as the Principal of Miramar Christian School. When he resigned from this role, he renewed his teacher's registration for a further three years, with the intention of working locally in a part-time time capacity. Education has always been his passion. He loves the day-today interaction with children and his colleagues and knows he's made a difference to some of their lives. Reflecting back, he said, "teaching has been a magical, fulfilling experience". He appreciates that he has had, and still enjoys, a very rewarding career.

In semi-retirement Kevin has taught part-time at Our Lady of Kāpiti School in Paraparaumu, worked with international students at Ōtaki College, and assisted the Boards of several NZ schools to make their most important decisions - the appointment of a principal. Currently, he works four days a week at Kāpiti College.

Kevin is delighted that so many of his ex-students remain in touch with him. Among them is Al Brown, Chef, TV Presenter, Writer and Restaurant Owner, who when reminiscing about his youth told Kevin, "Every day I just loved going to school. I'm entrepreneurial as a result of a year being taught by Mr B". During the COVID-19 lockdown (2020), Kevin received a phone call, out of the blue, from a medical student, who had been a pupil at St Michael's. She was writing an assignment about the first five people she'd expect to meet in heaven. "Unbelievably, I was one of people she had picked", he said. "When her father died, I brought the whole school to sing at his funeral, and she had never forgotten this. I was deeply touched when she contacted me and told me how she felt. She said that each day, at School, she was uplifted by my musical input and stories".

Apart from his teaching commitments Kevin is currently the Secretary of the Kāpiti Rotary Club. During the COVID-19 lockdown period, while walking around the neighbourhood, Kevin noticed the teddy bear displays that people had set up on their properties to help relieve the isolation and entertain the community. This experience sparked an idea for a children's book entitled 'The Magical Moments of Mr Bear', which he subsequently wrote. The book is illustrated with photos of the bears and includes a CD on which he plays the guitar and sings the 'Teddy Bear's Picnic' song. This book has brought so much joy to children and adults alike during what still remains 'the challenging global health crisis of our time'. Copies of the book have been given to local Pre-Schools/Schools, the Prime

Minister's daughter, and have also been sent overseas. Looking to the future he intends to write more children's books and has started writing his family history.

Reflecting on his 50-year career in Education, Kevin said, "It's an amazing and deeply satisfying achievement. To this day I still love teaching, especially my favourite subjects', History, Music and Maths. We are told that there are probably two teachers in our lives, who have put 'their brushstroke over us'". For Kevin, it was his Form One teacher, "Miss Ramsay, who set and instilled high standards of learning", and J.L.N Moore, his Form Five English Teacher, "who inspired with a unique teaching style of delivery by demonstrating Julius Caesar's 'Friends, Romans, countrymen' address whilst standing on a desk"! He said, "Mr Moore was the reason I went teaching. His favourite statement was 'if all else fails, read the instructions!' – it's so abundantly meaningful"!

Most of all Kevin is immensely proud of his wife Dianne and his three adult children. Amelia manages a boutique hotel in Russell, Bekky a talented musician is a Lighting/Sounds' expert for local Wellington theatre, and Ben is a successful Radio/Television personality as a member of the Jono and Ben partnership.

Dianne and Kevin with Sir Stirling and Lady Moss,
after Moss had opened the Tony Shelly centre at Scots College.
Tony, a Scots Old Boy, had also been a Formula One driver.

Kevin presents a $5,000 cheque, from Christchurch Rotary Club
to the Minister and Secretary of Education in Nauru and the Principal of
Nauru College

Kevin with his children, Amelia, Bekky and Ben

Four granddaughters, Sienna, Ayla, Indie and Skylar

JIM AND DERELEY BARRY

Jim and Dereley met at a New Year's Eve dance held at the original Foxton Beach Boatshed. Recalling the event Dereley laughingly said, "It was 1962, I was only 16 years old at the time. At the dance, there were two guys I fancied. I told my friend; I'll proposition the one that asks me to dance the Gay Gordon's". Twenty-three year old Jim Barry turned out to be the lucky guy!

Both Jim and Dereley were raised in the Manawatu, although they had quite different family backgrounds. Jim lived at Mount Lees Station where his father was a farmer. Jim and his three siblings all went to Mount Biggs School, "sometimes we walked, biked or all four of us together rode to school on a horse barebacked"! From the age of six Jim was doing general farm work. He said, "growing up on a farm I learned all the skills; milking, sheep farming, shearing and fencing". As farming was in his genes, he left high school aged 15 to start his first job at a farm 15 kilometres from his home. Jim's ultimate goal was to buy his own farm, and he needed to figure out how he was going to do this. In the mid 1950's, every farmer had sheep as wool was a desirable commodity. In the season, good sheep shearers were in high demand and could earn good money. Jim seized this opportunity and with his brother Rob, they started their own sheep shearing business. "We were known in Feilding and the surrounding area. Our reputation spread, and we became one of the biggest contractors in the district". The first year Jim entered the Golden Shears competition, aged 22, he won third place in the New Zealand Juniors event! The shearing business was so successful Jim bought his first farm (17 acres) when he was only 23 years old.

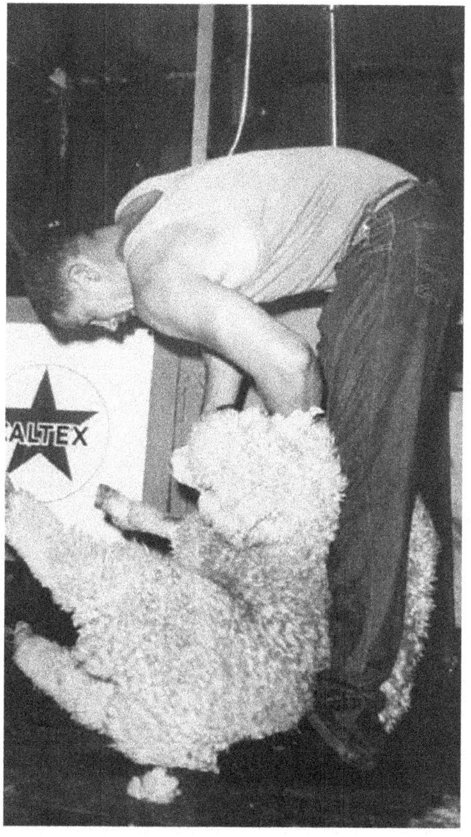

Jim at the Golden Shears competition held in Masterton.

Dereley, a love child following a wartime romance, was raised as the only child of her adoptive parents in Feilding. A bright child and talented artist, she attended St Joseph's primary school and continued her education at Feilding Agricultural High School where she became Head Girl. In her spare time, she enjoyed ballet and tap dancing, piano lessons, drama, and elocution and speech training had a huge influence on her life. As a teenager she regularly enthralled audiences with her humorous solo performances at various functions and started her own private speech practice while still at school. Passing her preliminary entrance exams, Dereley was accepted into Elam School of Art in Auckland. But she changed her plans and went to Palmerston North Teachers Training College instead, where she furthered her drama and art skills and experience. Studying close to home she enjoyed writing and performing humorous monologues and acting in plays at the Feilding Little Theatre, a skill she has shared with her students throughout her teaching career.

Living in close proximity to one another, Jim and Dereley's romance blossomed. They married three years after they met, at St Brigid's in Feilding, just steps away from Dereley's home.

Jim and Dereley's wedding (1965)

The couple began married life on Jim's farm. Dereley recalls, "the property had an in-ground outside toilet – it was a long-drop, and the washhouse was outside as well". While Jim farmed and managed his shearing business, Dereley taught speech. A year later (1966), Jim recalls a proud moment when he met U.S.A. President Lyndon Johnson. It transpires that he, along with his brother Rob and friend and co-worker Laurie Trembath, were selected to demonstrate their shearing skills at an exhibition organized for the President when he visited New

Zealand.

In due course Dereley and Jim started a family with the arrival of their son Scott. Seventeen months later their twins Trina and Todd were born. In those early years, the couple worked long hours and saved hard. Their tenacity paid off as they were able to purchase a bigger property at Mount Biggs (180 acres) and leased another 220 acres on an adjourning property while they were both still in their 20's! Just a week before their eldest child started school the family moved into the bigger farmhouse on their new property at Mount Biggs.

Mount Biggs was home to the Barry family for the next 42 years during which they were an integral part of the community. Their children, including Brad, their fourth child, all attended Mount Biggs School – it was the hub of the community and the same two-teacher country school that Jim had gone to as a boy. When their youngest child was 10 years old, Dereley worked at the school where she managed the Boards administration, ran programmes for children with reading difficulties, took drama, and taught swimming. She and Jim were heavily involved in fundraising activities to build the community hall.

Jim at one of the social events held in Mount Biggs Community Hall

Leveraging her creative strengths Dereley formed the 'Pink Club' for women. She wrote and coordinated a pantomime for adults and facilitated weekend art festivals and community themed woolshed parties.

Reminiscing she said, "a favourite night was the 'Invisible Ball' - we had so much fun hosting this event under a tarpaulin roof at the school"! She subsequently wrote short sketches and full length pantomimes for over 30 years and made sure every child was involved. During these years Jim chaired Mount Biggs School Committee and was a member of Feilding High Schools' Board of Governors. When the district needed a Justice of the Peace, Jim took on the role – a position he held for 20 years. A keen rugby fan, Jim was a member of the Manawatu Rugby Union Junior Advisory Board and coached schoolboy and teenage rugby teams for nearly 30 years and coached the Manawatu Under 21 and Manawatu Colts. Feilding's Amateur Swimming Club also played a big part in their lives. Dereley was a swimming instructor for 15 years and became the President, Jim was an official on race nights and the couple were awarded Life Membership of the club.

Growing up, Jim and Dereley's children learned farm skills from a very early age. With the passage of time Jim managed the farm and his shearing business with his brother. Recalling those years Jim said, "in the early days you got more for the wool than you did for the sheep, but over the years the reverse happened - land value increased, whereas sheep were less of a commodity". Nevertheless, Jim rolled with economic and environmental change, and took advantage of the opportunities as they became available. Whilst running his shearing gangs (with a staff of up to 100 in season), Jim farmed the 400 acres. Within five years the couple purchased 240 acres in Halcombe and bought the land they were leasing. In the early 1970's Jim held a four-man shearing Gang Record of 1,757 lambs! Over time, he employed staff on the farm, changed his focus and became a stock trader, buying in stock, shearing off the wool and then on-selling the meat to abattoirs and butchers. Mindful of the economic changes Jim was always careful to manage the risk saying, "we lived on a frugal income to service the mortgage and always paid our staff".

For decades Dereley and Jim led very busy lives, with very little time to pursue their hobbies. As they got older, Jim experienced some health issues. After two hip replacements he needed time to recuperate. Looking ahead, he wanted to spend more time fishing, gardening, and enjoying the beach. Dereley wanted to get back into her artwork, an activity that had been put on hold when the children were younger. As a couple, they both wanted to spend more time with their eight grandchildren and make sure they were around to see them grow up. Having made these decisions, Dereley and Jim began to make lifestyle changes. Fourteen years ago, they subdivided their farm. From part of these sales, they purchased a house at Foxton Beach in close proximity to Feilding and Levin, communities they were familiar with. Although their farm at Mount Biggs was their primary home, they gradually cut back on their work commitments and cultivated the hobbies they enjoyed. Dereley said, "I started taking Fridays off and went to paint at Foxton Beach. For the first time I took part in an Arts Festival". They also began to develop a network of friends at Foxton Beach.

When Jim retired eight years ago, aged 73, the couple sold their farm at Mount Biggs and moved to their home at Foxton Beach. At their beach house Jim has plenty of room for his 4 wheel-drive U.T.V., and he has the time to do the hobbies he enjoys - off-roading along the beach, fishing, white baiting at the estuary and gardening. Dereley joined a book club and the local Rebus Club where she coordinates the club's social events. Now she spends a lot more time painting fun art using acrylic and pastels.

Dereley has also written, illustrated and published a children's book called "Top Bottom Secret Undies Cover Agent", - a Stripey Blue adventure. Although the tale of Benny Boy's undies after he left them behind at the end of his holiday was written for children aged five to nine, adults also enjoy the story. Encouraged by her book's success, Dereley plans to write another – so watch this space!

Returning to Foxton Beach where they originally met, life has come full-circle for Jim and Dereley who have now been married for more than 55 years. While they maintain regular contact with their friends and family in Feilding and Mount Biggs, they have also developed a network of friends in and around Foxton Beach. This is where they plan to spend their retirement years, close to their four adult children, who incidentally have followed in their parent's footsteps – three are teachers and one became a farmer! They also have more time to enjoy their eight grandchildren.

Dereley with one of her paintings 'Three Beach Girls'.

'Godwit Flight Path'

Stylized family portrait

This book can be purchased directly from the
author. Contact dereleybarry@gmail.com.

Jim and Dereley, celebrating their 53rd Wedding Anniversary

MIKE ELLIOTT

Mike the oldest of six children was born in Te Pōhue, a small settlement in Hawkes Bay in 1944. The family moved to Oratia, a suburb of West Auckland so that his father could work in the orchard owned by Mike's grandparents. As the two families lived next door to one another, they spent quite a bit of time together. Mike went to Oratia primary school then on to Henderson High School, but the experience wasn't a happy one. He said, "I never wanted to go. I didn't enjoy school and couldn't wait to leave. I wanted to be an orchardist". Not surprisingly he left school at 15 years of age. As there wasn't enough work on his family's orchard, he went to work as a labourer pruning and spraying trees on a neighbouring orchard. While working there, Mike boarded with his employer's family. He only stayed six months as it became clear that the orchard was a 'hobby job' for the owners. Their main occupation was buying used tyres that required re-conditioning/retreading, which was common practice back then as they were in short supply in the late 1950's. During this period Mike went into service stations to buy the old tyres. He recalls, "I got two shillings and sixpence (2/6d) for each tyre" that he sold.

When this job came to an end, Mike returned home. Changing direction, he secured a job as a Toll Operator in the Auckland Telephone Exchange. Describing the role Mike said, "It was shift work and back then everything in the exchange was on cords. Everything was done manually. It's hard to imagine now. After 6pm, people in New Zealand had to book their toll calls, and because no one knew how long they were going to be on the phone, some people had to wait up to three hours for their call to be connected! Back then, the fee subscribers paid for those calls were charged for every three minutes. This is before New Zealand went decimal, so the fees were paid in pounds, shillings and pence"!

Around this time Mike's parents sold their orchard and moved to Gisborne. Mike's father took on a job as an orchard manager in Gisborne and while Mike's parents worked at a local orchard, they also bought a ten-acre block with the intention of turning it into their own orchard. To be closer to his family, Mike requested a transfer to the Gisborne Telephone Exchange as a Toll Operator (shift work) and joined them in 1963. The plan was that Mike, who was still keen to be an orchardist, was going to run the family's orchard and he and his mother worked hard to plant the orchard by hand. Unfortunately, just after the planting had been completed, Mike's father was diagnosed with lung cancer and had to have a lung removed. As his father was seriously ill and unable to work, there was no income, and the family still had the younger children living at home. Heartbreakingly the family had to sell half of their land - five acres, to a neighbour. As the remaining five acres wasn't big enough to pay its way as an orchard, Mike had to rethink 'where to from here'!

Considering his options Mike decided to remain with the Post Office. Embarking on a career path he sat the internal exams and at 21 years of age became a Clerical Cadet. Gaining experience, he was transferred to the Engineer's Office (phones) in Napier in 1966. By this time Mike had met and married Sarah, and the newly-weds initially made Napier their home. Their first child (Graeme) was born in Napier in 1967. In the years that followed Mike worked his way through the ranks and the family moved around the country with his job. The couple's second child (Veronica) was born in Greymouth, and two more children (Elizabeth and Michael) were born in Wellington.

While living in Greymouth Mike and Sarah had a traumatic experience when the Inangahua Earthquake occurred on the West Coast in May 1968. The earthquake, measuring 7.1 on the Richter scale, severely damaged many of the buildings. Three people were killed, and three more died in a rescue helicopter accident at that time. Mike remembers walking downtown and seeing a whole wall on the Royal Hotel had collapsed onto the street. The Japanese Rugby team were staying there at the time. He recalls, "It was a really frightening experience".

In his late 30's, while living in Wellington, Mike had a health scare. At the time he was a smoker, drank and played golf with his buddies, when one day he ended up in the coronary care unit in Wellington Hospital. "The doctor told me that if I didn't change my lifestyle I wouldn't last until my 45th birthday! It was a huge shock. I never smoked another cigarette. I bought a pair of running shoes and started running. The first time I went out I ran from the Post Office Headquarters in Wellington to the ferry terminal and back, a distance of three kilometres. I couldn't believe it – I had to stop six times to get my breath back. It was a lesson to me. From that day on I took my physical health and fitness very seriously". He entered his first marathon in Rotorua in 1979 and became so interested in the sport that he coached others, some of whom ran in New Zealand champs. Mike ran a total of four Marathons, the best of which was in Whanganui in 1984 where he ran the distance in 2 hours 46 minutes. Mike said he had to train hard to get results as he was not a natural runner.

Amidst all of this, Mike and his wife's relationship was struggling. After being married for 19 years, the couple went their separate ways. Graeme, Mike's eldest son lived with him for a short while when he was renting a Post Office House in Makara.

Photo taken outside the Beehive at the start of the Kāpiti Harrier's Wellington to Paraparaumu relay along the horse and cart route (now Transmission Gully). Mike, as the first runner is holding the baton. Margaret Shields, the MP for Kāpiti, is on the far right.

Around this time the Post Office, which was New Zealand's biggest employer, underwent major changes. Between 1985-86 the organisational and management structure was reviewed, and the subsequent report called for 'sweeping changes'! The organisation's three core businesses; New Zealand Post, Telecom New Zealand, and Post Office Bank Ltd., were set up as independent State Owned Enterprises. Mike was appointed Administration Manager of Telecom Wellington, which included Human Resources (HR), Logistics and Security with Telecom – combined, this was a significant portfolio.

In 1987 Telecom went through a second change with the establishment of Regional Operating Companies. Jim Harrison, who was the Regional Manager of Telecom Wellington, was appointed as Chief Executive of Telecom Central in Palmerston North. When Jim offered Mike the HR General Manager's role with Telecom Central, he eagerly accepted the position as this was an opportunity to establish HR systems and processes with a brand new company. To put this into perspective, this was when the functions of the traditional 'Personnel department', which were essentially administrative, radically changed to Human Resources (HR), which was a completely different occupation. In the 'new world of HR', employees were recognised as important assets, decisions about staff impacted the bottom line and customer service, and health and safety came to the fore. Mike and his new partner Lyn relocated to Palmerston North and bought their first house together. In 1988, Mike took up cycling. "I was in my 40's and by nature a very competitive person. I joined the Palmerston North Cycling Club and really pushed myself".

In early 1989, Mike's boss, Jim Harrison, moved to Christchurch to take on the Chief Executive's role of Telecom South. As he and Mike worked well together it wasn't long before he got a call from his former boss to join him in Christchurch. While delighted to be offered the Director HR role at Telecom South, (and with that came the appointment as an Executive Director on the Board), accepting the role meant that Mike and Lyn would have to leave their home that they just bought in Palmerston North. But this was a really great career opportunity. Mike applied and was appointed to the role, and with that he and Lyn moved to Christchurch, which was a complete change for them. Settling in Christchurch they both embarked on a whole new learning curve. Lyn took up a nursing career in the Spinal Unit of Burwood Hospital and Mike spent the next four years managing change. Telecom South covered the whole of the South Island, so it was a huge area and a massive undertaking for Mike. Reminiscing Mike said, "In terms of the change, Telecom South had lingered behind the other four Telecom Operating Companies".

In the coming years there was huge social and economic change in New Zealand. During this time Telecom was privatized. Subsequently the organisation underwent further massive structural and technological change between 1989-1993. Recalling these years Mike said, "Telecom reduced the number of its staff from 8,000, to less than 5,000 employees. My role as HR Director was very hands on. It was a very stressful time. The telephone exchanges were closed, as the technology was changing so rapidly. The motor vehicle workshops were closed because these were not perceived to be core business anymore. Although these were challenging times, I am very proud of how they (Telecom) looked after the people who lost their jobs. The organisation helped staff in the vehicle workshops in Timaru, Greymouth, Nelson, and Invercargill to get them loans and training to help them set up and open their own workshops. Furthermore, these businesses were given contracts to repair Telecom's vehicles for a minimum of three years".

In effect the philosophy of the organisation had changed, as it did in industry elsewhere. "It was a totally different ball game. Gone were the days when the people who used the services were just telephone subscribers. These were now customers, the most important people in the world, who were vital to the organisation's success. This concept, to be effective, required a significant cultural shift within Telecom". Leading the change, Mike initiated customer service development programmes to educate the staff. Telecom also embarked on the introduction of a quality improvement programme. Quality circles were initiated as Telecom strove to achieve the highest level of recognition for performance excellence as recipients of the Malcolm Baldridge National Quality Award. Mike was proud of the fact that by this time he was the only ex-Post Office employee in a Senior Leadership Human Resource role.

In 1991, Lyn and Mike tied the knot. They liked living in Christchurch, they enjoyed their jobs, and Mike was an active member of the Hornby Cycling Club. Although they had no plans to move, further changes occurred in 1992/93 when all of the Telecom companies were collapsed into one. It was a whole new world for Telecom with many redundancies. Mike was sent to Wellington and tasked with a massive project to set up one centralised payroll system for the company plus a centralized Security system - then he too was made redundant. Mike had been with the Post Office/Telecom for 32 years. It was the end of an era. Mike said, "there was no farewell function as by this time everyone I had worked with over the years had left the organisation"!

Following his redundancy Mike took time out. Exhausted, he spent three months recuperating at the couple's new home in Lower Hutt – but during this period he kept up his fitness regime. Having joined the Wellington Veterans Cycling Club, he generally cycled a minimum of 40 kilometres on a daily basis, and at least 100 kilometres on the weekends. He said, "I was much more successful at cycling than running". He achieved two NZ age group titles, was placed third in one other, and he won several medals at the Masters Games including at least four gold! Mike has also been in several crashes in races involving broken bones, but as he said, "Those crashes certainly paid for themselves"!

Mike cycling in Christchurch

Mike was awarded a gold medal for cycling in Invercargill.

Mike eventually accepted a role with the Capital Coast District Health Board (CCDHB), as the General Manager HR. As a Crown Health Enterprise, (CHE) this organisation had a high political profile. During the four years Mike worked for the CCDHB, huge changes took place, among them a new Nursing Clinical structure was implemented, and a new payroll system was introduced – both of which were major and quite stressful projects for those involved. During this time Mike cycled daily from his home in Maungaraki (Lower Hutt,) to the hospital and home again. When the next round of changes occurred within the health sector, Mike was made redundant for the second time.

Mike Elliott and Jim Harrison
This illustration captures their professional relationship and careers together.

Rather than take on a senior management role within a single organisation, Mike made the decision to go contracting, and secured significant and interesting contracts with the Ministry of Fisheries and New Zealand Defence Force. In 1999 he was offered, and reluctantly accepted the General Manager HR role with the Public Prison Service - one of the three major services within the Department of Corrections. At that time there were 18 prisons in New Zealand (with more than 10,000 inmates), and a huge number of staff, given that it's a 24 hour a day, 7-day-a-week operation. This organisation was also undergoing significant change in terms of inmate management and rehabilitation, and technological change. It was a tough environment to work in – one of the most difficult and challenging environments Mike had ever experienced, and one of the most complex in terms of the people involved.

During this period in his life, Mike used some of his redundancy money to purchase an 11 hectare orchard in Ōtaki. So, at long last, Mike had achieved what was for him a boyhood dream. He continued working in Wellington and employed an orchard manager to assist with the running of the orchard. Mike also did a lot of work himself on the orchard. However, at the time the apple industry was going through lean times, and orchards in the Ōtaki area were not as productive as those in Nelson or Hawkes Bay. Unable to sell the orchard as a going concern, Mike and Lyn pulled all of the trees out and burnt them, and then they sold the land, along with the house that they had built. Although he loved working on the orchard, it just came at the wrong time in his life. Mike and Lyn lost quite a bit of money with this venture, but they gave it a go and have no regrets.

Mike resigned from his job at the Public Prison Service to become a part-owner and Director of HR Solutions as he'd always wanted to own his own business. In the years that followed he enjoyed contracting with multiple organisations in the greater Wellington Region. Life was pretty good – and then in 2008/9 the global credit crunch hit, the share market dropped and there was a severe downturn in New Zealand's economy. Consulting contracts were scarce, and HR Solutions went into voluntary liquidation. Mike and Lyn suffered huge personal financial loss, including the loss of their home, and by this time Mike was in his 60's. Looking back on these times Mike said, "It was really stressful – but as Lyn said, we still have each other".

Mike has an incredibly strong sense of character, is extremely motivated, self-reliant, and resilient. Drawing on these strengths, and with Lyn's support and encouragement he secured an Employment Relations role with New Zealand Transport Agency. Four years later he moved on to the Employment Relations and Principal HR Advisor's role with the Ministry of Health where he worked until he retired in 2016, at 71 years of age. While at the Ministry of Health Mike had another heart health scare which resulted in him having a pacemaker implanted. This also spelt an end to his cycling career. However, Mike continued managing cycling races for the Wellington Masters Cycling Club, that included organising a two-day tour – an event he managed for 10 years.

After an incredibly interesting career spanning more than five decades, Mike and his wife Lyn relocated to the Horowhenua. Initially he undertook casual contract work with local organisations, providing them with HR expertise. Now he works in a voluntary capacity with the Citizen's Advice Bureau and Age Concern in Levin. In recent times he was diagnosed with prostate cancer. As he works hard to maintain his health and level of fitness in later life, he has made a good recovery. To this day Mike cycles on a regular basis. "I've had lots of crashes on my bikes over the years. Now I'm not as competitive and use an e-bike"! In Mike's world, his wife and their relationship and attitude to life is everything. In his words, "I've been very lucky. Meeting and marrying Lyn was the best thing that ever happened to me. My father, who died when he was relatively young, was a very special person in my life as was my mother".

Mike's parents

"I can recall my mother watching me cycle race in Whanganui in 1994 when I was involved in a large serious crash, which she witnessed (as did Lyn). I suffered a broken collar bone and shoulder blade and I lost a significant amount of skin. I spent a night in hospital. She never watched me in a cycle race again"!

Mike has been disappointed that some of his children have not been as close to him as he would have liked. Regardless, he still loves them as much as he ever has. He said, "I don't believe in the word retirement. People don't retire, they have lifestyle changes". Reflecting on his life Mike said, "I've had a full life and never shirked from trying things. Not everything has turned out right and I have made some costly mistakes on the way, but I have very few regrets".

SOLVEIG MIKKELSEN

Solveig Elisabeth Mikkelsen (Liz), the oldest of five children, was born on a farm in the far northern tip of Denmark during the second world war. In those days few people had cars – people either walked or cycled or got around in a horse-drawn carriage. Solveig said, "I can remember riding my bicycle to the grocery store when I was six years old. At 11 years of age, I rode my bicycle eight kilometres to and from school every day in all kinds of weather". Due to her parents' financial situation, Solveig left school after having attained High School Certificate. After undertaking several casual jobs, she was engaged by Smeds Bus Linier, a large bus company where she completed an apprenticeship in accounting involving evening classes. Solveig said, "I was so lucky to have this experience, and the skills I learned set me up for life".

She met Klaus, her future husband while working in Copenhagen. Klaus was exceptionally bright and a very talented mathematician. As newlyweds, given their qualifications, skills and experience, the couple qualified for assisted immigration and, after going through the process, they emigrated to Australia in 1969. They settled in Melbourne, and although they were more than 14 thousand kilometres away from their families in Denmark, they loved it, especially the sunshine and warmer climate. During the seven years they lived in Melbourne their two children Thomas and Daniel Skipper were born.

In 1976, when Klaus was offered a job in New Zealand, the family moved to Wellington where the children went to school. Some years later the couple went their separate ways - Klaus left his family to work in America while Solveig chose to stay in New Zealand with her children. In the coming years Solveig worked part-time to support the family, and during this time the family's primary means of transport was their bicycles – they cycled everywhere.

In the early 1980's, tertiary training establishments in New Zealand encouraged mature individuals with work experience to enrol in further education. As a single parent raising her boys, this opportunity appealed to Solveig, so she enrolled in a Teachers Training programme at Karori Teachers College in Wellington. As it was too far to cycle back and forth to teacher's college each day, she bought a little motorbike. Solveig graduated with a Trained Teachers Certificate in 1985. At 44 years of age, she began her teaching career at Eastbourne Primary School in Wellington and later taught at Hutt Intermediate School for two years.

Meanwhile, Solveig kept in touch with her parents and siblings in Denmark. The family made trips back to Denmark to visit them when they could, and Solveig's parents and sister came from Denmark to visit them in New Zealand. As with many families who emigrate, the children were raised to be bilingual. Over time emigrants adjust to new ways of living and most stay in contact with loved family in their homeland. Solveig said, "handwritten letters were a joy then, both for my mother and myself, and best of all my mother kept all my letters, which told about our adventures and daily life in New Zealand. These letters have become our treasured family story".

Solveig and her sons held family conferences at which they made decisions on matters that impacted them as a family unit. In 1986 they discussed whether they should live in Denmark for a while. This would give the children the opportunity to immerse themselves in Danish family life and culture, and a chance to be near their grandparents, aunts and uncles and enjoy their love. The impetus for flight was another failed marriage in late 1986. During that same Christmas holiday period, Solveig and her sons went on an adventurous bicycle trip cycling from Lower Hutt to Christchurch. It was a trip that helped to heal wounds and created a bond between the children and their mother.

Early 1987, Solveig gave up her job, sold the family home and she and her two sons, who were then aged 12 and 14, excitedly set off on the trip of a lifetime. First, they went to Melbourne for a couple of weeks, so the children could see where they were born. Leaving Melbourne, they flew to Athens in Greece and went on to explore Crete and The Peloponnese – places that were steeped in history, and where Thomas and Daniel could eat baclava - a sweet they really loved! Sailing to Italy the boys met up with their father on the Spanish Steps in Rome and then the family spent some time travelling through Italy. Highlights of their time in France were their visits to Avignon and Paris. Heidelberg in Germany followed. In Cologne they bought a tiny green second-hand Renault car and three bicycles which they loaded onto the roof.

Arriving in Denmark the boys eagerly looked forward to seeing Legoland, the original Lego factory in Billund, Jutland - the largest tourist attraction in Denmark. "This was an amazing experience"! Solveig recalls, "we arrived in Denmark in June. The children couldn't believe that it was still light at 11 o'clock at night". It took the family two months to reach their family in Denmark. Reminiscing Solveig said, "It was a real adventure".

While in Denmark, the family lived in Sindal in North Jutland, close to Solveig's parents and where the children went to school. Solveig, who is fluent in Danish, German and English, had secured a teaching job at Hjoerring Private Realskole for one year, and later taught at a state school. Recalling the experience Solveig said, "the New Zealand education system was, and still is, highly regarded overseas. Kiwi teachers have a very good reputation. I taught German, English, Social studies and singing". She laughingly added, "I was also supposed to teach sports, but instead introduced walks through the countryside for the children". The family lived in Denmark for two years. Although Thomas, her eldest son would have been happy to stay, Daniel and their mother missed life in New Zealand, especially their friends and the outdoor life. While it was a wrench to leave their Danish family behind, Solveig and her children made the decision to return to New Zealand to live.

Back in Aotearoa, Solveig and her sons settled in Lower Hutt and later Wellington where she eventually bought an apartment of her own. She initially did some relief teaching, but after a while decided to return to her first occupation - accounting. While the children finished their schooling, Solveig worked for several different companies where she installed accounting systems and trained the employees in how to use them. Solveig also finished the degree she had begun at Victoria University through correspondence with Massey University in 1995. It was during this period in her life that she started to write in her spare time and was overjoyed when one of her short stories, 'Bicycle Courier Wanted', was published in the School Journal (Part 4, No 3, 1995). Wellington's terrain is very hilly, cyclists share the busy city streets with general traffic – trucks, cars, and motorcycles as well as the trolley bus system that was fully operational throughout the city until 2017. When her boys left home, Solveig found she had more time on her hands. Looking for a way to contribute she searched for a group of people that she heard were campaigning for cycle safety. She met Celia Wade Brown, one of the founders of the 'Cycling Advocate's Network' - later renamed Cycling Action Network (CAN), and became a member of the group. In due course this advocacy group became a national voice for people on bicycles in New Zealand. Collaborating with like-minded people they worked with government, councils, and businesses to plan and create an integrated, safe cycling environment, and promoted the benefits of cycling to the nation. Solveig became a very active member of CAN and managed the organisation's accounts on a voluntary basis for 10 years. She also joined a Toastmasters Club to develop her public speaking skills enabling her to talk with confidence at cycling conferences.

Aged 58, Solveig began a whole new chapter in her life. Selling her apartment, she relocated to Ōtaki, on the Kāpiti Coast where she bought a small house on beach property. Solveig, who had always loved gardening said, "it was here my dream of creating a special garden became a reality". Seeing the potential, she created a garden on three different levels.

Over the next 10 years Solveig commuted from Ōtaki to her job in Wellington. Cycling the five kilometres from her home to Ōtaki Railway Station, she boarded the 'Capital Connection' train into Wellington and did the same trip in reverse at the end of the day. "It kept me fit throughout my 60's" she said. When Solveig arranged to have a cycle commuter locked box shifted to the station, it wasn't long before other people began biking to the station, as they too could store their bikes safely each morning and then get on the train for their first cuppa.

In 2001, after returning 'home' from a visit to her family in Denmark Solveig was made redundant from her job. She tried to get another job, but at 60 years of age it was difficult. This was compounded when the employment agencies insisted, that she didn't have the right qualifications! "Actually, I had lots of qualifications and I decided to use some of them". Refusing to accept their comments Solveig took responsibility for herself. "I constructed a portfolio of my skills, did some advertising then set out on bus, train and bike to reach companies who wanted to learn Excel, Access and Word. It wasn't always easy, but it mattered to me that I could use public transport and my bicycle. Sometimes, if it rained, I would go for coffee and then change in the toilet. I did this for a year after which I got a part-time job, three days per week at an architectural firm in Wellington. This was the best job ever because it gave me time for the garden and for bicycle promotion".

By this time Solveig had formed Kāpiti Cycling Inc., (KCI) a cycling advocacy group set up to promote and improve cycle safety on the Kāpiti Coast. When the local Mayor, Alan Milne, voiced his concern for Kāpiti's environment in 2002, he invited walkers, horse riders and cyclists to a public meeting and Solveig went along. Subsequently a group called Cycling, Walking and Bridleways (CWB) was formed to advise Council. KCI facilitated a programme to actively encourage Intermediate and High School students to cycle to and from school, rather than use other means of transport. The campaign was very successful. Students at Paraparaumu College began to cycle from Waikanae over the footbridge to school. With the help of volunteers, the students created a film about this project which was shown at several events. Later Solveig wrote a column on cycle safety for the local paper in Ōtaki. It wasn't long before a leisure cycle group began with two women friends. Solveig said, "we met every Tuesday morning for a bike ride and then went for a coffee together at a local café". The idea took off as the recreational group rapidly expanded in numbers and now more than 40 men and women regularly take part in this activity.

In association with the Council and the Rotary Club of Ōtaki, KCI was instrumental in securing funding for the construction of the beautiful pathway for pedestrians and cyclists at the foreshore on Paraparaumu Beach. This is part of the coastal route between Paekakariki to Ōtaki, begun in 2002. "Sadly, for those of us who fought for it, the Kāpiti Coastal Cycleway and Walkway came to a halt at Te Horo Beach Road. Other Ōtaki residents helped to connect the Ōtaki River Pathway to Te Waka Road, which meets the State Highway 300 metres North of Te Horo Beach Road. Alas, 300 metres of dangerous road for cyclists to negotiate!"

When Solveig retired from work at 70 years of age, she made a conscious decision to write her life story. "I wanted my grandchildren to know about their family in Denmark and about my childhood. I also wanted my family in Denmark to know about my life in New Zealand". Inspired by the "demanding but invaluable course" facilitated by writer and playwright Renee Taylor, Solveig subsequently spent several years writing her memoirs. One of the greatest things a family member can do is to write their story, it's a treasure for those involved and a legacy for future generations.

At 70 years of age, Solveig met a new partner and together the couple planned a trip of a lifetime. They travelled to the United States to visit Solveig's son Thomas at his dream home by a beautiful lake in Holliston, Massachusetts. Solveig said, "I had been many times before, but this time it was good to go exploring together on my son's bicycles. Sometimes Carter, my grandchild would join us". One of the highlights of the trip was to cycle across the Golden Gate Bridge.

Leaving the United States, the couple continued on to Holland where they searched for and bought the famous 'Brompton' folding bicycle for her husband in Amsterdam. Later Solveig bought a 'Giant' folding bike in Denmark. She recalls, "how good it felt to be 'home' again meeting my brothers, sisters and cousins and their partners". The couple went to parties, took trips to small islands and "went on drives in my brother's car to interesting places in my own country. We also used our folding bicycles on short family trips".

After spending four weeks with her family the couple boarded a train to Berlin where they "cycled through the city on lovely wide roads allowing us plenty of space and we visited all the important spots". A highlight was Berlin's main railway station with its elegant, spacious, shops, restaurants, and a huge, beautiful forecourt. Reflecting on this experience she said, "in the railway stations in Europe travellers are looked after in every way - as good as air travellers! In New Zealand we are waiting in cold open spaces with facilities lacking in comfort and nothing but draughty cafés and crowded toilets. Why is it that train travellers do not deserve the same comfort as air travellers?"   Moving on, the couple visited Prague through which the Witava River flows, before catching the train to Italy. Solveig said, "the bikes were allowed on all trains in Europe and provided us with our own transport when sightseeing". In Italy they walked the Cinque Terre trail; Solveig recalls, "it was so beautiful. The tiny towns along the way where we could rest and eat were a delight". They also explored Sienna, Florence, Bologna and finally rested for a week in a small friendly hill town called Loiano.

Solveig's adult sons now have families of their own and she is delighted that her grandchildren aged six, nine and 11 all love to bike. "Returning to New Zealand I continued my career as a grandmother, regularly taking the train and buses to my son's home in Wellington to look after Finn-Oskar, Sven-Aksel and Helene Francis. They also enjoyed spending their holidays playing at the beach".

Solveig, now in her late 70's, recently sold her Ōtaki home. Mulling over the decision she said, "it was hard to leave, but the property was getting too big for me to do by myself". Her husband had moved on to greener acres, while she moved into a new home in Masterton "where everyone is friendly, and everything is easy and available within a bicycle ride". Throughout her life Solveig's passion for cycling has never wavered. Her passion has also rubbed off on her family as her youngest son Daniel owns a Bike shop in Wellington, and she manages his accounts for him. She has three bicycles of her own - an electric bike, a folding bike and an ordinary bicycle and regularly rides them all. The electric bike replaces the car, because she can carry big loads and go further - even at 78 years of age. She especially enjoys the Monday morning Women's group that cycle together in the beautiful Wairarapa Valley. She said that during the COVID-19 lockdown (2020), research showed that respiratory illness declined. Coincidentally, one of the positive outcomes of the lockdown was that there were fewer cars on the road. This resulted in cleaner air, fewer road accidents, and many more people were out on their bikes in the fresh air!

Solveig has written two books. "The Cycle Train", an illustrated children's book promotes safe cycling to and from school in groups. She said, "the concept is similar to the walking school bus. It's important that parents are confident their children can ride their bike safely and trust them to cycle to school by themselves". Her second children's book is called "On Our Bikes, The Long Route South".

Both of Solveig's books are available from Paper Plus bookstores in New Zealand, or can be purchased directly from the author liz.ocean@gmail.com. When asked what's next Solveig said, "I am hoping to be of some help to the District Council to turn Masterton into the Cycle Town of the Wairarapa" - so watch this space!

Solveig's garden

Solveig cycling on the Golden Gate Bridge

Solveig on her e-bike in Masterton 2021

Solveig (Liz) Mikkelsen's books

Solveig (Liz) Mikkelsen

MAUREEN TAYLOR

Maureen was born 18 months before the outbreak of the Second World War in Southend-On-Sea. Southend, is a large coastal town in southeastern Essex, England, located just 64 kilometres east of central London on the north side of the Thames Estuary. As it was wartime, much of Maureen's early life was spent in the Anderson shelter - the air-raid shelter that was built into the ground in the family's back garden. She vividly remembers the layout, "it had a three-quarter size bed with a couple of bunks overhead for my brother and I. There was a chair and two poufs to sit on, a small oil stove and a cupboard to store a saucepan, cocoa and a few tins of food". When the sirens went off, people would dash to the shelters.

Maureen remembers, "most evenings about 6pm, we went to the shelter in our pyjamas. We had a story and practiced our reading and went to bed in our bunks, so we were already there when the sirens went off. My older brother Bernard and I would huddle up with Mum and hear the planes fly overhead on their way to London. We could tell which ones were the British planes and which were the German planes by the sound of the engines. Sometimes they would drop the bombs on their way back and these mainly fell into the mile of mud as the tide receded". She also remembers the buzzing sound of the doodlebugs – the V1 and V2 flying bombs, that exploded on impact creating death and destruction on a massive scale. "When we heard these, we were scared, but when the sound stopped, we were petrified. When this happened, we quickly threw ourselves down on the floor and Mum laid on top of me to protect me. These were scary times".

In wartime, many parents were reluctant to send their younger children to school as the bombing attacks occurred day or night. Adults and children alike were fearful when the sirens wailed to signal danger was approaching. Maureen's mother kept her children close to home as much as possible and was even more cautious when Maureen contracted a bout of pneumonia. Maureen recalls, "it was my Mum who taught me to read, write and do math's in our air-raid shelter. She also taught me how to knit and how to sew dolls clothes". During the war years, while much of the adult population were in some form of service either in the home country or overseas, families did the best they could to raise their children in terrifying and unpredictable circumstances.

Maureen was seven years old when the war ended. "V.E. day was unbelievable. Curtains were pulled back and lights were on – I hadn't seen this before as the blackout had been in place all my life. People got dressed up and went out – even at night, something we hadn't done before. Mum, Bernard and I walked down to the seafront"! This must have been a spectacular experience as Southend's pier - the longest leisure pier in the world and a major landmark in the area, was taken over by the Royal Navy during the war.

Maureen went to Bournemouth Park Road primary school and later attended Southend High School for Girls. She was the baby of the family until she was 10 years old, "so it was a bit of a shock when my baby brother Robin came along - suddenly I became the big sister". Maureen and Bernard who was four years older, were very close.   "Bernard belonged to the Southend Youth Group, and under his care, I was allowed to go on trips with him from time to time. It was a real treat".

In 1951, as a teenager Maureen went on a trip to Switzerland with the youth group. This was a very big deal in the days when few families took holidays overseas. "We travelled by coach from Southend to Dover where we, along with our coaches, boarded the ferry to Calais, then there was the long journey by coach to Switzerland. We stayed in chalets near Grindelwald and visited other towns and cities. We saw bananas - a fruit none of us younger ones could remember seeing before! The chores were rostered, and we all did our fair share. We slept in our sleeping bags on a bed of straw. It was great fun". Maureen recalls, "the trip cost £30. As children, we were taught very early on that we had to stand on our own two feet, so I had a paper round to earn the money to go and Mum and Dad topped up the shortfall". In 1953, the youth group travelled to London for the Queen's Coronation. Maureen said, "everyone was so excited and dressed up for this momentous event. It was great fun; I have never forgotten it".

When she left school, Maureen worked at the haberdashery counter in Dixon's Department store in Southend. A few months later she went hairdressing, a job she really enjoyed. When Maureen was 17 years of age, she and her family visited her dad's brother in Prince Albert, a small town in Saskatchewan, Canada. While there she secured a hairdressing job. When it came time for the family to return to England, Maureen decided to stay in Canada for 12 months with the promise that she would return home to Southend in time for her older brother's wedding. "I loved it" she said, "I learned to ice skate. I saw the Northern Lights and fantastic electrical storms, and I learnt how to fire a rifle and a pistol"!

Fulfilling her promise Maureen returned home to her family,

and soon after she met her future husband George, a Heating and Ventilation Draftsman from London. In 1961, the couple began their married life in two rooms in Islington in the heart of London, and in June the following year, their first child Mark was born.

In the early 1960's skilled workers were in high demand overseas. Assisted immigration schemes were introduced to support families to migrate to commonwealth countries such as Australia, South Africa, Canada, and New Zealand. A chance to get ahead in a warmer climate appealed to George and Maureen and they made the decision to emigrate to New Zealand. In due course their application was accepted, and they and their 17-month-old son Mark boarded the SS Himalaya passenger liner bound for the southern hemisphere. It was tricky managing their toddler during the five-week voyage Maureen said, "he was like grease lightening up on the rails around the ship. We had to restrain him as he was so fast, or he would have been up and over them and into the sea"! During this voyage, the news of President Kennedy's assassination was announced. "Everyone was stunned, a hush followed and for the rest of the day voices were muted" she said.

When the SS Himalaya docked in Auckland on Friday 27th December 1963, the family boarded the overnight train to Wellington. As a young Mum one of the first things Maureen noticed in Aotearoa was how well fed the babies looked. "They were so much fatter. In post war London the milk in the baby's bottles was watered down to keep the babies slimmer and heathier as the smog made breathing difficult"! Remembering her first impressions as they chugged along on that trip, "the air was so clear and fresh – there was no smog! The landscape was so much more mountainous than I had anticipated".

Most of the shops were closed when they arrived in Wellington on a Saturday morning. In those days weekend trading was virtually non-existent, and shops and businesses traditionally closed for annual leave during the peak summer holiday period. "The local dairy was great. They lent us a saucepan, a can opener, some plates, and cutlery. On the Sunday morning we went to a service at Wellington City Salvation Army. They made us feel so welcome and lent us bits and pieces until our trunk came down from Auckland nearly six months later! The family settled in Wellington where George's job was located, and within a couple of years their second son Paul was born. Maureen said, "life here was so different to what I had been used to. The people were kind and welcoming".

Sometimes life doesn't work out as we had planned. When George and Maureen's marriage broke up, the couple went their separate ways. Raising the boys on her own Maureen realized she couldn't afford to stay in Wellington. She relocated to Levin in the Horowhenua "because it reminded me of Prince Albert in Canada where I had lived as a teenager. Levin is a small friendly town where everything is available. When I moved into my home in Arapaepae Road, my neighbour, Jessie Prouse was especially kind to me and my children. I remember the first Wednesday I was there; I heard the wail of a siren. It shook me. I raced to pick up the children from the garden, but I didn't know where the shelter was. It wasn't an air raid – it was the alarm calling for the volunteer firefighters to deal with the event! It seems funny now, but it was so real at the time. The lifestyle was so different in a small town compared with the city".

Time passed, and the family settled in Levin. Through the Salvation Army Church, Maureen became friends with Alice and George Dowd. It was they who introduced her to Buster, George's partner in a Plumbing, Gasfitting and Drainage business named 'Dowd and Taylor'. Buster and Maureen got on well together and gradually started to see each other on a social basis. Their relationship blossomed and they tied the knot on her 31st birthday in March 1969. The newly-weds set up home in Levin. In June 1970, their son Andrew was born followed by their daughter Johanne, 17 months later. The baby of the family Shirlene was born three years later.

In the years that followed, Buster had plenty of work, and their five children flourished along with their much loved pets - Blackie and Sooty, their cats, and Paddy their Samoyed dog. In his spare time Buster developed a garden and Maureen liked to knit, sew, and read. During these years, the family had a caravan and enjoyed weekend and school holiday trips at various locations around New Zealand. In the early 1980's, Buster and Maureen went to England to spend time with her elderly parents, and following her mother's death, Maureen successfully persuaded her father to come and live with them in New Zealand.

When the children were growing up, Maureen had more time on her hands, so she got a part-time job at the local maternity home. It was around this time that she and her friend Greta began to attend evening classes at Horowhenua College where they could learn new crafts such as woodwork and basket-making. One of the classes that Greta became interested in was patchwork and quilting. Maureen reluctantly went along to the class and to her amazement fell in love with it, to the extent that she has maintained and enjoyed this creative hobby for more than 30 years!

When Buster retired, he and Maureen had more time to enjoy holidays in their campervan. Maureen said, "everywhere we went people were so friendly". Casting her mind back she recalls, "We were enjoying a campervanning holiday in Tauranga in 2001 when we heard the horrific news about the attack on Twin Towers in New York. Everyone was horrified"! While on this holiday the couple made the decision to spend their retirement years in the Bay of Plenty and relocated to the sunny beach suburb of Papamoa in December 2001. Settling into their new environment Buster enjoyed his gardening, Maureen joined a quilting club and they both joined the Omanu Probus Club which became a big part of their lives.

Within a year Buster became Vice-President and the following year was the President of the Probus Club, a position he held for two years. They had no trouble making new friends in the area, but they always remained in contact with their family and friends in Levin and Australia.

Sadly, Buster died five and a half years after moving to Papamoa. The couple had been happily married for nearly 40 years. In the days and weeks that followed family and friends were very supportive, and gradually Maureen adjusted to living on her own. Her Probus friends persuaded her to join the committee and she subsequently became the President of the club. Maureen stayed on in their family home in Papamoa for a further five and a half years before she made the decision to return to Levin to be closer to family and friends. "At that time two of my children were living in New Zealand, and three were living in Australia. Buster's niece and family were in Levin and over the years I'd kept in touch with our friends in the Horowhenua". Maureen's friend, Frances Clark lived in a retirement village in Levin. "When I visited her, I liked the look and feel of the place. I was lucky to get a sunny villa of my own in this community – it just felt right". On reflection Maureen said it took about 12-18 months to adjust to her new surroundings. She has never regretted the decision. As she said, "If I need to chat with someone all I have to do is walk over to the Recreation Centre. It's a meeting place with a café and there are always people around, so you never need to be lonely".

Seven years have passed since Maureen moved back to Levin. Now in her early 80's, Maureen enjoys a social life both in the village and in the wider community. She has maintained her driving licence and values her independence. She also enjoys holidays both in New Zealand and overseas with family and friends. During the COVID-19 lockdown, when social distancing restrictions were in place, Maureen made good use of the time. Focusing on her creative talent she made a beautiful alphabet themed patchwork quilt for her great grandchildren living in Australia to share. Over the years she has made and gifted several quilts and wall hangings. Maureen's favourite themes are roses and cats. She said, "I've always been a cat lover. My cat Millie is very special, she is so loving and such good company".

Maureen has five adult children eight grandchildren and four great grandchildren. Four of her children now live in Australia, and luckily, two of them came to visit Maureen in New Zealand just prior to the COVID lockdown. She is looking forward to seeing them all again once the restrictions have been lifted. Her youngest daughter Shirlene lives close by in Levin. Maureen said, "she is so good to me" and she appreciates the time they spend together. Looking to the future, Maureen has recently started a new project. She is documenting her memories to share with her family and friends.

Maureen, Buster, and their family

Maureen and Buster

Maureen and Buster with some of the grandchildren

The 'Bear Family Album Quilt', hand appliqued and machine quilted was donated for a raffle. The proceeds were given to Waipuna Hospice in memory of Buster Taylor.

Maureen and her cat Millie

ALISON MERWOOD

When Alison and her husband Kevin were planning their retirement, they looked for a home in a safe and comfortable environment where they could maintain their independence. While they wanted to belong to a community, Alison said they also wanted, "to be able to shut the door and go away motorhoming in our van 'Roughing it Smoothly' whenever we felt like it without having to worry". At the time, the couple were living in Papakowhai a few kilometres north of Wellington. They had looked at villas in several retirement villages before settling on a show home in a fairly new retirement village in the Horowhenua that fitted with their lifestyle. In 2004, Kevin then aged 66, and Alison aged 64, sold their house in Papakowhai and moved into their new home in Levin.

Alison was born and raised in Lower Hutt and on leaving school went to Gilby's Business College in Wellington. When she graduated, she worked in a legal office in Wellington until she got married. She met Kevin, her future husband, at a dance at St Francis church hall in Wellington. She vividly remembers, "he was wearing a pale blue sports coat and our eyes met". Eighteen-year-old Kevin was in Wellington for the weekend for a Billiards tournament. Rather than join his friends in the pub after the game he chose to go dancing instead. Kevin and Alison got chatting and when the dance ended, he offered to take her home, but Alison said no as she had agreed to go home on the train with the friends she had gone to the dance with. Kevin lived and worked on his family's sheep and cattle farm in Taihape nearly 200 kilometres away. Not wanting to lose contact with one another Alison recalls, "he wrote my name, address and phone number on the back of a used railway ticket, and after that most of our courting was done in letters".

In 1956, the South African Rugby Union, commonly known as the Springboks, toured Australia, and New Zealand. They played a series of matches throughout New Zealand and one of these was held in August at Athletic Park in Wellington. Kevin's family made the trip south to see them play. Alison was invited to join them explaining - "this was our first date". Kevin's father picked Alison up from her home, after he collected his other son Noel from St Patrick's College in Silverstream where he was a boarder. Recalling the event Alison said, "it was a freezing cold day on the Northern Bank of the stadium, with no seats - standing room only, with a strong southerly wind blowing straight into our faces". It was a momentous occasion as that weekend Kevin also met Alison's parents for the first time.

After that first date, Kevin wrote to Alison inviting her to stay with his family in Taihape for Labour Weekend at the end of October. Her parents wouldn't let her go, as they didn't know this family and, after all, Taihape was a long way away. Luckily Kevin's grandparents lived in the Hutt Valley and the next time he and his family visited them, they invited Alison and her family around to meet them. When the day came, everyone got on so well together that Kevin's mother asked Alison's parents if they would allow her to visit for Labour Weekend. After meeting the family, including Kevin's younger sister Mary who was the same age as Alison's younger sister, her parents were reassured their daughter was in safe hands and allowed her to go.

Alison clearly remembers the family farm and the homestead

where Kevin lived. It was situated six miles from the centre of Taihape at the end of a country road. Alison said, "it broke his parent's hearts when the Public Works Department built State Highway 1 straight through the middle of their farm, dividing it into two separate sections, literally splitting it right up the middle, ruining the property and making it difficult to farm. It was never the same again".

Kevin and Alison couldn't get married unless they had a house to go to. Fortunately, Kevin applied for and secured a shepherd's job that came with a house on a 6,000-acre station at Pukeokahu. The couple got married in February 1960 and moved onto the farm straight after their honeymoon. For Alison it was a very different life to the one she had been accustomed to in the city – but she loved it. "The farm was 26 miles from town on a dirt road – if you saw two cars a day, it was exciting". Kevin worked as one of the shepherds and Alison's job was, "to provide breakfast and morning and afternoon tea for the boys. I baked a batch of scones every morning. It wasn't long before I could bake them with my eyes closed". As a farmer's wife she said, "I was supposed to ride a horse on this hilly farm, but I was never confident, so I drove the Land Rover instead".

Peter, their first child was born 18 months later during a terrible storm. Alison said "the weather was so bad it took hours to get to the maternity hospital in Taihape. Word got around on the telephone party line that I was on my way into town and the local farmers came out and cleared the road in three different places to enable us to get through". While Kevin drove the car, Alison said "I had to put my hand out of the window to keep the wipers going as the snow was coming down thick and fast. Then we got stopped by a Traffic Officer who tried to help us. The roads were so slippery it was very frightening. We had to get out and walk the last part of the trip and got to the hospital at 11.45pm". Peter was born in the early hours of the next morning. "The storm was so bad Kevin had to spend the rest of the night at the hospital. It was two days before we could get word to my parents as the phones were down and even the ham radios weren't working"!

From a very early age Kevin was very good with his hands and loved woodwork. He built cowsheds, woodsheds, gates and did all kinds of jobs around the farm. Thanks to a family friend who was Managing Director of a big construction company in Wellington, Kevin was offered a job, which he accepted. Ultimately, he worked on many of the major buildings on The Terrace in Wellington and, over the years, he rose through the ranks from Labourer to Site Manager.

After the family relocated to Wellington, following a troublesome pregnancy, Nigel their second son was born prematurely in 1963. Nigel was severely handicapped and subsequently he spent years in Kimberley Hospital. Deeply distressed it was a very difficult time for the whole family. The couple had always wanted four children but having another one of their own was just not possible, and eventually they made the decision to adopt two more children. Alison and Kevin were overjoyed when their applications to adopt were accepted. Lynette was welcomed into their family in 1965 and Brenda came three years later.

While the children were growing up Alison was involved in their school committees. When Rewa Rewa School was built in Newlands, she took an active role on the committee to establish the school's administrative system, and readily accepted the role of Secretary to the newly appointed Principal. On leaving Rewa Rewa School she helped a friend in her public typing and employment agency in Lower Hutt.

During the school holidays the family borrowed a caravan that belonged to Alison's parents. They loved the freedom this type of holiday offered and they met so many other families who were having fun along the way. It wasn't long before they made the decision to buy their own mobile holiday home, appreciating this would give them the opportunity to enjoy more time travelling around New Zealand, camping outdoors, while at the same time enjoying many of the comforts of home. After doing their homework they settled on a mini mobile camper that was a trailer with a hood and an awning. Kevin made a purpose-built unit to go inside that had cutlery drawers and cupboards for the pots and pans. They joined the Wellington Caravan Club and began a tremendous adventure with the children. Every month they'd take part in a caravan rally somewhere in the country, often meeting up with motorhoming families in school grounds. Over the years the Merwoods spent their weekends and holidays having a fabulous time towing their mini mobile camper to destinations all over New Zealand.

When the children had grown up and left home, Kevin yearned to fulfil his dream to build his own motorhome. After doing their research he and Alison bought a 25-foot Mitsubishi bus with 25 seats in it. They could see the possibilities and embarked on a project to convert it into the motorhome they named 'Roughing It Smoothly'. It took Kevin two years to convert the bus. Remembering the experience, and the end result Alison said, "it was absolutely beautiful". The couple's inaugural trip in 'Roughing it Smoothly' was undertaken in February 2000.

During these years the couple also organised several international motorhoming trips for club members. Highlights were the trips they made to the United States and the United Kingdom. Along with 12 other couples they toured the western states of the United States for four weeks in 1997, and in 2000 they toured the United Kingdom in a convoy of 22 motorhomes for four weeks. "We had a fantastic time travelling around exploring the roads, towns, and the landscape, and met up with the locals along the way – it was great fun"! As these trips were reciprocal with members from caravan and motorhoming clubs overseas, the Merwoods often coordinated and hosted hospitality tours for visitors to New Zealand in association with the Wellington Caravan Club.

As previously noted, Alison and Kevin took 'Roughing it Smoothly' with them when they relocated to Levin in 2004, but sadly Kevin died 12 months later in 2005, aged 67. Following his death, their motorhoming friends were very supportive, "they formed two guards of honour at Kevin's funeral" said Alison, and they kept in touch with her in the months and years that followed. Although Alison had so many happy memories of the wonderful trips they had made in holidays in 'Roughing it Smoothly', the motorhome was too big for one person, and in due course she made the decision to sell it.

Nevertheless, Alison's motorhoming days were far from over. She said, "lots of women go caravanning on their own", and fortunately she had developed a wide circle of friends over the years who shared the same passion! With the help of her network in the motorhoming community, she looked around for a little motorhome that would meet her requirements. One day the call came from good friends in Auckland who had spotted a vehicle that seemed just right for her – an ex-Kea rental. Alison made the trip to Auckland to have a good look at it. The vehicle was a two-berth "with all the mod cons for example a toilet, fridge, a stove and was very comfortable". It was perfect – just what she had been looking for, so she bought it. At 66 years of age, Alison took to the road in her new motorhome she named 'Kevali' – an acronym for 'Kevin and Alison'.

As a single woman, she continued to enjoy wonderful motorhoming holidays all over New Zealand with her friends for the next 11 years. Alison was 78 years old when she finally made the decision to sell 'Kevali'. She is delighted that the couple who bought it changed its name and two years later they still have it.

Alison recently celebrated her 80th birthday with her four children, six grandchildren and nine great grandchildren. A social person, she has developed a wide circle of friends in the retirement village. She joins in all of the activities, plays croquet, and looks forward to the monthly social events held at the village. Alison, who has lived in her villa for 16 years said, "it's a wonderful place". A member of Probus and the Music Society she also enjoys a social life outside of the village.

Alison and Kevin's Motorhome 'Roughing It Smoothly'

Alison and Kevin

Alison with 'Kevali'

KEN ALLAN

Ken was born and raised in Canada. As an adventurous young man, after much planning, he set off on a trip to see the world in 1959 aged 22 years. He said, "I was travelling alone. I chose New Zealand as my first port of call as it's a Commonwealth country and we spoke the same language"! Ken, who has always been physically active, looked forward to exploring both the North and the South Island. "On leaving Aotearoa I planned to travel to Australia and then on to India. Back then I had no idea that I would make New Zealand my home".

Within two years of arriving in the country, Ken met Maureen in the South Island. Maureen was raised in Te Kuiti and was brought up on a marae where everyone knew everyone. Although she and Ken came from quite different backgrounds, the couple were the same age, and shared similar interests. Maureen, the mother of two young children, became the love of his life, and three months later, the couple got married in Petone Methodist Church. The newly-weds settled in the Wellington region and expanded their family straight away. Reminiscing Ken said, "No birth control back then! We had four children in quick succession - a baby every year for the first three years, then 18 months later a fourth child, so we had six children altogether". Initially the family lived in a small state house unit in Taita. Later, they were able to capitalise on the family benefit to put a deposit on an ex-state house, and immediately set to work to renovate it to meet the family's growing needs.

Ken puts his all into everything he does including his work, family life, his hobbies, and his exercise regime. He became the

Chairperson of the Home and School Association; a Defensive Driving Instructor and was a keen photographer. He took up cake making and cake decorating when he and a friend attended an evening class together. Taking this hobby seriously, he handmade and hand-painted his daughter's 21st birthday cake. The following year he facilitated the cake decorating course himself! In 1974, he forfeited his Canadian citizenship and surrendered his passport when he became a New Zealand citizen. As he said, "In those days, dual citizenship wasn't an option"!

Ken's career spanned several decades. He finally retired on his 75th birthday. Reflecting back, he said, "I enjoyed going to work, always starting work early and finishing late". In every role he undertook, he made sure that he provided tip top value-added service. "My last two jobs, each of 16 years duration, were very fulfilling. I think that is because I was able to mould the jobs around myself".

The first of these two jobs was with TVNZ at the Avalon complex in Lower Hutt. Ken's portfolio of responsibilities included all non-production activities (e.g., accounts, records, transport, properties, and security). One of the highlights he recalls was when he worked on the '24-hour Telethons'. These highly successful, live nationwide shows were among the biggest television events held at the time. The shows featured local and international talent that appealed to adults and children alike. With the support of the general population these events generated huge sums of money for charitable causes. Little did the nation know that behind-the-scenes, Ken managed a staff of 623 volunteers on the Telethon weekends, including cadets from St John Ambulance, and security services to facilitate 3 x

8-hour shifts to make this happen. Everybody loved this event and to this day many remember the song associated with it *"Thank you very much for your kind donation"* New Zealand Telethon 1981 - YouTube Ken was very involved with St John's Ambulance, and became the Honorary Vice President of Taita branch. He also supported their National Competitions that were held at the television studios, which resulted in him receiving an award.

The St John's Wellington District Award - presented to Ken,
for his outstanding assistance with the organisation of their National Adult
Competitions.

On leaving TVNZ Ken spent the next 16 years working with the Ministry of Foreign Affairs and Trade in Wellington. Here he undertook a variety of administrative roles managing records and files within several of the divisions with this organisation. Given the nature of his job, his sharp organisational skills, and his friendly, helpful, outgoing personality, he developed a wide network of relationships within Foreign Affairs, across government agencies, and with the diplomats and staff working in the various embassies and consulates in New Zealand. Ken could seamlessly access the right people and pertinent information because he knew the system inside out and was familiar with how the service worked. As a result, he was recognised as the 'go to' person when people were looking for specific documents and the paper trails relating to historical policy decisions.

Ken has always maintained a rigorous health and fitness regime and particularly enjoyed jazzercise, yoga, and swimming. A keen long-distance runner, at 47 and 48 years of age he ran five full marathons, always leading with the fast pack completing these events in two and a half hours.

As the years passed, the family grew up and left home. Looking to the future Maureen and Ken began planning for their retirement. They purchased a family home in Paekakariki and relocated to the Kāpiti Coast where the couple spent much of their free time remodeling and refurbishing their new home and planting out their garden. Just as the renovations had been completed tragedy struck. In January 2001, Maureen, who had suffered from migraines for much of her life, died suddenly of an aneurysm. It was a huge shock and Ken was devasted – "Maureen was the love of my life. It was a marriage made in heaven".

Maureen and Ken

Following Maureen's death life was incredibly difficult for Ken. "We were both 63 years old when she passed away and had been together for 40 years. After investing $50,000 renovating our Paekakarirki home, I couldn't bear going home after work. One month after Maureen's tangi, I joined the Les Mills gym which was next door to where I worked. I was with people doing something physical. It was so good for me". Reflecting on their lives together Ken started to sort through more than 600 family photographs and became interested in preserving their family history for their children and grandchildren. He researched both Maureen's and his own genealogy/whakapapa. Amazed at what he was learning, he systematically began creating the family tree for each side of their family and collated the various documents and photographs into a series of manageable artistic projects. "I started with our parents and then our grandparents and looked into how I could display the photos and documents with the written detail for the family". Consumed with the project, he methodically compiled a series of 27 beautiful albums as a legacy for his family. For Ken this was a labour of love and a way of dealing with his loss.

Although Ken loved their home in Paekakarirki, he didn't want to stay there without Maureen. He sold the property and moved to Waikanae where he volunteered with Age Concern and Neighbourhood Watch. Seeking further development, he completed a 10-week course with the Widowed, Separated and Divorced support group. Ken said, "This course was so useful. I did so well at it that they asked me to facilitate the next course, which I did. I was a Facilitator and a Guest Speaker for various courses until 2018". Finding these development opportunities helpful he enrolled in a Landmark course. Impressed by the experience, he paid for his daughter and her husband and three children to complete this course as well.

The gym became a focal point in Ken's life, and he immediately sought out a personal trainer. He advises, "A good trainer is essential if you are going to get the best out of your exercise regime and get super fit". Ken had a go at everything that was available in the gym, including weights, and mastered the use of a Swiss ball to improve balance.

At 68 years of age, wanting to try something new, he took two extra weeks long service leave from his job and enrolled in an "Outward Bound Course" in the Marlborough Sounds. Outward Bound facilitates challenging outdoor activities for groups of people who want to extend themselves beyond their comfort zone. Ken, along with people who were much younger than he was, (in their 30's), had the opportunity to try out all kinds of activities such as tramping, kayaking, rock climbing, and high wire, to extend themselves in a non-competitive, supportive, safe environment. Ken said, "I had a go at everything. I tried sports I've never done before like kayaking and competed against myself. I even did the 16 kilometre walk up Mount Royal and the solo overnight experience in the bush. It was a fantastic experience". Age really is no barrier if we have the right mindset.

In his late 60's, Ken was a regular at Les Mills gym. Invigorated, he entered an event known as the Gut Buster, whereby the athletes run up and down 26 stories of stairs. A member of the International Security Division, Ken was the firecracker in the 2007 event, as he completed it in three minutes 15 seconds! He also entered the XTERRA Trail Running Series and finished up being the 15th person home, completing the run in 47 minutes 51 seconds. As he was the oldest athlete in this event, he was awarded free membership.

One day, while at the gym and quite by chance, Ken was encouraged to take up body building. Highly motivated he followed a strict diet, exercised at the gym daily, and worked with a personal trainer twice a week for eight months to achieve his goals. In September 2009, he entered and won the Over 50's body building event, which is remarkable given that Ken, was the oldest competitor. Winning the event was a proud moment for Ken and his family and although he gained automatic entry to the Nationals, he said, "I'd achieved what I set out to do and I didn't want to take this further". Subsequently, an article regarding this event was reported in the Dominion Post twice – before and after the event!

After Ken retired from work, he relocated to the Horowhenua where he's actively involved in the community and is a visitor for Age Concern. He's since had both hips replaced and having made a good recovery, he walks daily and swims six days a week. "I've always been a swimmer. It's absolute bliss. It's good exercise and nothing hurts! A while back I entered a swimming promotion and although two weeks late starting, within a few weeks I'd completed 3,058 lengths, (76.75 kilometres) in the pool. I won the lucky draw – a trip for two to Kāpiti Island"! On his 84th birthday he swam 84 lengths of the main pool at the Aquatic Centre in Levin. Not surprisingly, Ken has a biological age of a much younger man. He said, "I don't take any medication and, and have been a blood donor for 53 years – during this time I've made 61 donations"!

In later life family remains very important to him. Whenever possible he spends time with his four daughters, two sons, and his 13 grandchildren. To this day he manages his own home and garden and constantly seeks out new opportunities and challenges. Ken firmly believes that the only limits in life are the ones we place on ourselves. His motto is

"Use it or lose it"!

Ken on the Outward Bound course
in the Marlborough Sounds

Ken was 72 when he entered this event.

Ken, the oldest competitor, won the Over 50's body building event

HELEN DEW

Helen has always grown her own fruit and vegetables, and says, "I've always had a natural bent to conservation". Concerned about society's dependency on commercial food systems and the impact it has on climate change, she has taken massive action to encourage people to take personal responsibility and become more conscious consumers. Highly motivated, with stacks of energy and drive, she pursues her interest with "passion and persistence". At 81 years of age, Helen began hosting 'Edible Gardening' workshops at her home in Carterton. Her primary aim is to encourage the community to grow, eat and share healthy food, and thus reduce the carbon footprint involved in the current food production and distribution system. Her practical 'hands on' workshops are promoted to the community via her 'Garden for Life' Facebook page. At each event, she shows people how they can establish and maintain a productive low maintenance garden to grow their own vegetables, herbs, and fruit.

Helen, the first of five children in her family, was born in 1937 in Picton, in the South Island. At the time her father, (Jack), had a short-term farm labouring job in Resolution Bay in the Marlborough Sounds. The family returned to Wellington where they lived until Helen was eight years old. Then they moved to the Wairarapa, a rural area north of Wellington, where Jack worked on dairy farms in Carterton. Given the nature of Jack's work the family moved ten times in ten years and, as a result, it was difficult for Helen to form friendships. A shy child, Helen said she "felt invisible" at school, always on the side-lines, and "had little self-confidence and self-esteem". She left school at

15 years of age with no qualifications. Her very first job, was on the menswear counter at Woolworths, which gave her some independence. Shortly after, she secured the first general office and accounting role with T.F. Watson and Co, a large general department store in Carterton.

Helen met Alf Dew, her future husband, at a 21st birthday party in Carterton. She recalls she was only 16 years old when they met, and Alf was six and a half years older. The couple courted for four years, "we sold Alf's car and bought a quarter acre of land on the outskirts of town". They moved into their new home when they got back from their honeymoon and lived there until Alf's death.

Helen and Alf Dew

Soon after marrying, Helen left the workforce as this is what newly married women did in those days. Their first child, Paul, was born ten months later -three more children were born in quick succession (David, Clare, and Stephen). From the early days of their relationship, Helen and Alf shared a love of gardening and grew their own fruit and vegetables. Helen also enjoyed floral art and reading, but life wasn't always easy. As a young mother of four children Helen experienced a prolonged period of depression, which culminated in a nervous breakdown. Admitted to Porirua hospital, 84 kilometres away, she underwent electric shock treatment (electroconvulsive therapy) to relieve her symptoms. Although this was a necessary step, it was a very distressing and difficult time for the whole family, especially with no car. Helen said, "full recovery was a gradual process, over several years". Alf was tremendously supportive during this difficult period in their lives. Reflecting on her experience Helen said, "I'm delighted to be able to declare that, with the help of counselling, medication, family and community support, I'm a living example of enjoying a a full and satisfying life after mental illness". In her final session she presented her counsellor with this poem she had written.

To John, a Dove

Remember sparrow
with broken wing,
alone
with leaden heart?
From glass-walled fortress
watchful, wistful
while all about took flight

Anguished eyes searched vainly for release, pleading
weeping
met only life's heinous gaze
reflecting guilt, shame
pronouncing
doom

Anxious fear near sealed her in her tomb
Then Dove, with eyes of Love
looked fondly to her
warmly
gently
gifted her the key of trust

Window of his soul
shone deep, illuming hidden vaults
revealing - no - not faults
but gold
and gems, sparkling

Having begun life with little confidence or self-esteem, Helen said, "the biggest lesson I've learned in my life journey, is to let go of fear of rejection or judgment, and to welcome others into my life". Following her illness Helen gradually became very involved in the community and blossomed into a confident, outgoing personality. In 1991, concerned with social, economic, and environmental wellbeing, she and Alf joined the 'Wairarapa Green Dollar Exchange', a system that enables members to trade with a complementary currency. In 2002, she became a founding member of 'The Living Economies Educational Trust', an educational charity that provides information on "how citizen-led economic solutions can improve the community's wellbeing and contribute to a healthy planet". For more information see www.livingeconomies.org.nz.

As Helen's confidence and her network of like-minded people expanded in New Zealand and overseas, she attended international conferences addressing the flaws in the global economic system and promoting local and global community currency models. She was one of the presenters at a complementary currency conference in Hannover, Germany in 2003, and an attendee at a similar conference in New York in 2004. In 2004, Helen's service was officially recognised when she was the recipient of the 'New Zealand Orangi Kaupapa Trust Award', for her voluntary work in the Wairarapa and for pioneering complementary currencies in the region. She subsequently joined numerous other committees and community organisations including 'Neighbourhood Support' and 'Wairarapa Voice'. She initiated and coordinated a Café Forum in Carterton, and is a founding member of 'Wairarapa Timebank', 'Resilient Carterton', 'Carterton's Farmers' Market' and 'Savings Pools'. Helen's tireless commitment to service in her community over the years is virtually interminable. Between 2006- 2018 Helen managed the online bookstore for 'Living Economies'. She was the Project Manager for the NZ edition of the book "Fleeing Vesuvius — Responding to the effects of economic and environmental collapse" - a compilation of works by various writers published in 2011 by Living Economies. The aim is to "arm its readers with all they need to develop new ways of doing things, instead of staggering from crisis to crisis trying to patch up systems that are only suited to economies that can grow and grow."

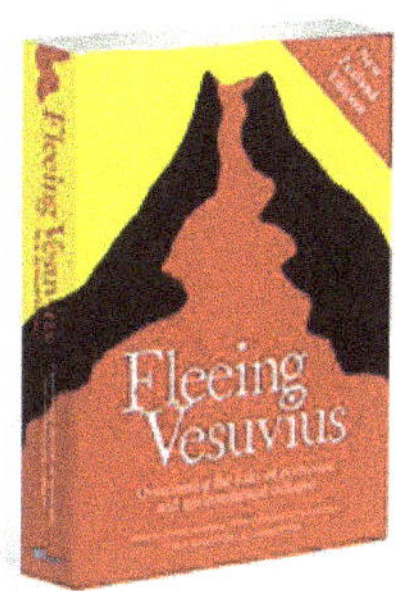

Available from www.gardentools.nz/living-economies-bookshop

In 2018, Helen was the recipient of the 'Charles Rooking Carter Award' for service to the Carterton community for an extended period of time. The same year she was the second runner up for the 'Wairarapa Senior Persons Award' celebrating the International Day of the Older Person.

Meanwhile, with the passing of time Helen and Alf's children grew up, left home, and had families of their own. In later life, Alf developed chronic bronchitis. Helen nursed him at home but sadly, after 57 years of marriage, aged 82, Alf died. Helen describes his funeral as being "more like a concert" as several family members performed at his service.

Following Alf's death Helen had intended to stay in the family home and continue to manage her quarter-acre section by herself but had to re-consider her plans when she had a slight stroke and lost her sense of balance. Initially she couldn't leave the house unaided, which was very frustrating and hampered her independence. Helen said, "once I got the right medication, I made a good recovery". While recovering from her stroke, Helen also suffered from 'restless leg syndrome', a condition apt to disrupt sleep. During these wakeful hours she considered her options – should she stay in the home she and Alf had shared, with its big section and so many happy memories, or should she move? Helen said "the answer came suddenly during the night" – it was time to downsize, after all she could take her memories with her and start a new life. Losing no time, she immediately got out of bed and reduced the content of her wardrobe by half. Still sleepless at 3am she repeated the exercise in the bathroom. At 80 years of age Helen sold the family home and moved to a tiny property closer to town. She immediately set up a productive garden where she hosts her workshops on edible gardening, compost-making, seed-saving, and pruning.

At the Charles Rooking Carter Awards evening, Helen met Lucy Adlam. Lucy had initiated a community organisation called 'Joy for Generations' to alleviate loneliness and reduce social isolation in the community. The vision is "for all generations to be connected, valued and included in our community", and they do this "by bringing people together in simple practical ways". The initiative began by bringing people together in rest homes, then the 'Stories for Generations programme' was established. The ideas flowed; people connected through musical sessions. As people appreciated the benefits, the organisation gradually expanded. A collaborative venture between the Council and the community resulted in the installation of a dedicated 'Happy to Chat' bench set up in a community space to encourage people to talk to one another.

Helen and Lucy became very good friends through their mutual interest in strengthening the community and they supported each other's projects.

Each year, the 'Women of Influence Programme' showcases stories of women who make a difference to the lives of New Zealanders. Sponsored by Stuff and Westpac New Zealand, the Women of Influence Awards "shine a light on the amazing work Kiwi women are doing from grassroots to the global stage". In 2019, Lucy nominated Helen for a 'Women of Influence Award' under the 'Community Hero category' for "her long-standing service to the Carterton community and her environmental initiatives encouraging sustainability and resilience". Surprised but delighted with the news Helen said, "honouring me with this nomination also honours the Carterton community. I've had the good fortune to have lived most of my life in a small town, where I've experienced the truth that it takes a community to raise a person of humble origins to become a 'woman of (a little) influence'. I've also been blessed with wonderful support from my late husband and our family, and I couldn't have wished for better employers as I began my working life at 15 years of age, with no formal qualifications".

Although, not selected as a finalist, Helen and Lucy made the decision to attend the Awards event in Auckland to celebrate and network with others. Incredibly creative, Lucy sought sponsorship for their rail travel to and from the event from 'Kiwi Rail's Great Journeys of NZ. In exchange, they piloted the 'Happy to Chat' concept in collaboration with Great Journeys of NZ, engaging their fellow passengers in the process. Helen said, "attending the Women of Influence Awards event, and the journey from Carterton to Auckland and back, were fabulous and memorable experiences for which I'm truly grateful", - what's more is that their fellow passengers also enjoyed the experience.

Helen, now aged 83, is very proud of her four adult children, 19 grandchildren and 23 great grandchildren. To this day she is an active member of many community groups, including Living Economies. She played a key role in a New Zealand award-winning documentary 'Living the Change', now available on demand. https://vimeo.com/ondemad/livingthechange. During the COVID lock-down Helen offered her 'Edible Gardening' workshops online, enabling the wider population to learn from her experience. Friends are currently working on an illustrated book for children of all ages, encouraging present and future generations to adopt sustainable lifestyles.

Looking to the future Helen says, "My work continues. A particular concern is the economic impact of COVID-19. I hope to have a local currency system adopted by all sectors of the community within the next year, to enable trading to continue in the wake of the anticipated economic downturn." Helen signs off with another poem:

The Tree and I are One

In Totara's roots
I'll live
grateful for Earth's nurturing
for kin and community
with hope
that seeds sown
will flourish

Helen Dew in the berry cage in her garden

Lucy Adlam (left) and Helen Dew on the 'Happy to Chat' bench

JIM AND JOAN BOLGER

Jim Bolger and his future wife Joan Riddell were both born and raised in neighbouring farming communities on the south-west coast of Taranaki. Although their families were known to one another, the couple actually met through the Young Farmers Club and the Country Girls Club. Jim was the lead debater in the Young Farmers Club, which was an important part of the club's social life. In 1960, the Rahotu team, with Jim as leader, had made it to the North Island debating final that was held in Palmerston North. At that time, Joan was training to be a teacher in the city, and she and her friends went along to cheer on and support the lads from Taranaki. Jim recalls, "the topic for the debate was designed to test inventiveness and provide fun and was: 'That animals should wear felt hats in the summer', and we put forward an opposing argument, not, as expected, that the whole idea was stupid, but rather that they should wear straw hats". The Rahotu team won the final and the couple's relationship developed from there. Three years later Jim and Joan were married in the Pungarehu Catholic Church situated on the rural southwest coast of Taranaki. Reflecting back on their lives together Jim said, "It was the best decision I ever made".

In 1935, James (Jim) Brendan Bolger, the third of five children, was born into an Irish Catholic family in Opunake. Jim's parents had immigrated to New Zealand in 1930 immediately after they were married. Their first job in New Zealand was hand milking cows on a farm in South Taranaki. Jim started school in Omata, south of New Plymouth, where the family had a small farm. Years later, he returned to the Omata School as Prime Minister to help celebrate the school's 125th anniversary. In 1941, the family purchased a slightly larger farm at Rahotu, 46 kilometres south-west of New Plymouth, so he completed his primary school years at the Rahotu school.

During the war and in the years that followed, there were few resources. Everyone had to pitch in to develop their farms and assist each other to get things done. Jim recalls he and his siblings often helped their mother milk the cows, and he and his brothers helped their father to dig the trenches to drain the gully swamps on their rocky, hilly property. As a nine-year-old, in the last year of World War 2, Jim was called upon to help out on a neighbour's farm. The neighbour, who was a World War 1 veteran, needed assistance while his son trained for the Air Force. Jim lived with the family and helped milk the cows before and after attending his lessons at Rahotu School. From that experience Jim went on to help several of the neighbours in the district with their milking, on a voluntary basis. In a way, this was the start of Jim's life journey of being prepared to become involved and to confront the status quo if that was necessary.

The Bolgers lived by a strong set of Christian values and attended church on Sundays. In what spare time there was the family were very keen readers of books from the small local library. Of course, they listened to the radio which, back then, with the daily newspaper, was the source of all current news. Jim's parents came from County Wexford Ireland, the same County that US President John Kennedy's family came from. The Kennedy family lived about 30 kilometres away from his Grandparents, who of course he never met. Jim remembers that his father took a very keen interest in the 1960 US

Presidential election as he saw Kennedy as 'one of them'. Jim said his interest in American politics started back then. In general, the family was very interested in local and international political issues.

Like many young lads, Jim also enjoyed playing rugby. He left Opunake District High School aged 15, which wasn't unusual in those days, to work on the family's dairy farm and established a small agricultural contracting business with his two brothers. In 1962, when his father died, Jim then aged 27, bought the family farm with the help of a State Advances Corporation loan.

Joan, the second of five children, was born in 1941. Similar to Jim, Joan and her siblings were raised in the Catholic faith. She attended Pungarehu School which was close to her parent's farm. The famous All Black Barrett Brothers also attended Pungarehu School and their grandfather was in the same class as Joan. The children from the nearby Parihaka Pa, which was invaded by colonial troops in 1881, also attended, but sadly consistent with the approach of the time, neither Jim nor Joan were taught anything about that terrible invasion and the confiscation of Maori land that happened in their neighbourhood. This was an issue Jim was keen to address much later when he was Prime Minister. Joan also attended Opunake High School for her secondary education. An aside, Jim points out that "the last three Members of Parliament from the Taranaki King Country electorate all attended the Opunake High School. Some record for a small school!"

Whilst some young women stayed in the rural community when they left school, others left the district to train as nurses and teachers. Joan trained as a teacher at the then Palmerston North Teachers Training College. Following her graduation, she went home to Pungarehu and taught in the same primary school she had gone to as a youngster. Joan took part in the lively social events in the district, and she also enjoyed debating. In fact, after the Rahotu team won the North Island final, Jim coached members of her Country Girls Club debating team.

Jim had been dairy farming all his life and had undertaken leadership roles in the Young Farmers Club and the community. After he and Joan married in 1963, Joan moved onto the farm and gave up her teaching role. "It was the end of an era" she said. Jim also looked towards the future and decided it was time for him to change direction and take on a new challenge. In 1965, the couple sold their Taranaki property and purchased a small sheep farm on the outskirts of Te Kuiti in the King Country. Jim had an affinity for animals and had always cared for his dairy herd. Learning on the job, he quickly got up to speed on how to manage a healthy sheep and beef operation in what was a different farming environment to the one he and Joan had been accustomed to.

In the late 1960's and early 1970's there were several droughts in the northern King Country. It was a tough time for farmers and their animals. This situation was compounded by the "endless strikes" in the meat processing industry, which had a huge impact on the farming community, and the towns that provided services to the community. For example, animals would be transported to the freezing works in various parts of the North Island and when a strike occurred, the stock could be stranded for several days before they were transported back to the farm again. Jim said, "it was cruel. Something had to change". He was visiting Joan after their second son Paul was born in Te Kuiti in 1966, when he noticed that Federated Farmers, a rural advocacy group, were having a meeting. He went along and joined the group.

A few years later, frustrated that little was being done to rectify the situation they all faced, Jim, with a group of like-minded farmers in the region formed a self-appointed 'Farmers' Action Committee'. This group organised several public meetings and invited politicians to come to the King Country to meet with affected farmers and see for themselves the disastrous conditions, with a view to encouraging them to return to Wellington and take steps to resolve the situation. Jim was appointed as their spokesman. Hundreds of people attended the first meeting in Te Kuiti. The invited Government speaker was Hon. Daniel Riddiford, the then Minister of Justice and Associate Minister of Labour. Jim spoke with conviction on behalf of the community, and as he said, it was the first time he was on nationwide television. People listened.

Subsequently other speakers including Labour leader Norman Kirk, who was a very powerful platform speaker, and Robert Muldoon, who was the Minister of Finance at the time, and union leaders were among those who visited the King Country to meet the farmers to get a first-hand appreciation of the situation, and importantly accept that change was necessary. Jim said, "most people find change frightening and the Unions, and the Meat Works owners were no different". Following the meetings Jim and a few other farm leaders proposed building a different meat processing works in the King Country, with the unions having a 20% share in the ownership so that they also had an interest in operating it on a sensible basis. Their group achieved the agreement of the Unions and gained the necessary financial support from farmers, but the meat processing industry was regulated back then. The group Jim was leading was not granted a licence by the Meat Board, so another approach to change the failed status quo was denied.

Given the many issues he had been involved in, Jim, who had not been particularly involved in Party Politics was approached by a large delegation from the local National Party and urged to seek the nomination as the National Party's candidate for the new King Country electorate in the upcoming 1972 election. There were six others seeking the nomination and he hadn't considered that career change. After all, he was now the Vice President of Waikato Federated Farmers and on the National Council amongst other things. Plus managing the family farm was a full-time occupation and by this time Joan and Jim had five children to consider. The couple talked it over, and, after much discussion Jim recalls that Joan said something like "if you think you can do some good then you better go and do it".

After a hard-fought campaign Jim won the nomination and he became the National Party's candidate in New Zealand's 1972 election. However, the Norman Kirk led Labour Party won the election and Kirk became the Prime Minister (PM). Jim entered the Opposition when he was elected the National Party's Member of Parliament (MP) for the new King Country electorate. Little did Jim know that he would represent his electorate in Parliament for the next 26 years!

Following the 1972 election, life for the Bolger family radically changed direction. As a backbencher, Jim worked in Wellington for most of the week for much of the year, so he and Joan appointed a manager to run their farm while he was away. Jim got into the rhythm of commuting between the King Country and Wellington - 440 kilometres each way every week to do his job in Parliament. Meanwhile, Joan remained on the farm with the children and fielded calls from his constituents as there was no secretarial support for MPs in their electorates back then! Jim embraced his new role and responsibilities. Quick and eager to learn, he rapidly came up to speed with a broad range of issues in the turbulent and changing political environment. He was also aware of the massive wave of technological change that was on the horizon and anticipated some of the potential challenges and the opportunities that would need to be managed, especially in the world of work.

Three years later at the 1975 election the political world changed again. Robert Muldoon, Leader of the National Party, became Prime Minister and Jim's responsibilities increased. Joan and their six children relocated to Wellington, which meant that Jim was able to spend more time with his family during the week and returned to the King Country at weekends to deal with constituency issues. In the coming years the Bolger family expanded with the arrival of three more children. Meanwhile, Jim's political career went from strength to strength.

In 1975, under Robert Muldoon's leadership, Jim was first appointed as Undersecretary to the Hon Duncan McIntyre, Minister of Agriculture and Fisheries and Maori Affairs. In this position Jim Chaired the Maori Affairs Select Committee which heard the petition that had been brought to parliament by the redoubtable Dame Whina Cooper just before the election. As the Chair, Jim decided that the Select Committee should sit in Auckland to hear the petition, addressed to all Members of Parliament, that "no further Maori land should be taken". The final words of the petition are "management, retention and control - of Maori land - remain with our people and their dependents in perpetuity." A framed copy of this hangs on the wall at Jim and Joan's house.

Jim Bolger with Dame Whina Cooper.
Backstage at the Chase Stadium – final rally 1987

Signing the Heads of Agreement, Tainui Settlement,
With Maori Queen Dame Te Atairangikaahu

A key feature of Jim's term as Prime Minister was the considerable effort, he with other colleagues made to push forward Treaty Settlement's to resolve some of the gross wrongs from New Zealand's early colonial era. Jim has continued his interest and work on Treaty issues up until today.

In early 1977, Jim was appointed a cabinet minister, as the Minister of Fisheries and Associate Agriculture. In this position he pushed forward, with the Hon. Brian Talboys, (the Minister of Foreign Affairs; Overseas Trade and National Development), the 200-hundred-mile exclusive fishing zone to give New Zealand the fourth largest fishing zone in the world and the beginning of New Zealand's modern fishing industry. Following the 1978 election, Jim became the Minister of Labour and continued in that position until the 1984 election, and for a period, he was also Minister of Immigration. As Minister of Labour, he was elected President of the International Labour Organisation (ILO) in 1983. The ILO is older than the United Nations and had a larger membership of countries. The ILO's annual conference has equal representatives from the Government, Unions and Employers and is held in Geneva. The conference's primary purpose was to discuss labour laws, workers' rights, and the general status of workers' conditions across the world, but back then, during the 'cold war' between the West and the Communist controlled countries, international politics was never far from the surface. The conference lasted four weeks and Jim said he and Joan "enjoyed exploring Switzerland on the weekends with the car and driver supplied for the President's use".

Although the National Party was defeated in the 1984 and 1987 elections, Jim's leadership was very highly regarded in his electorate. As a result, he retained his seat in Parliament for the fifth and sixth consecutive terms. Jim became the Deputy Leader of the Opposition in 1984, and before long he became the Leader of the National Party. In the 1990 election, in the biggest landslide victory in New Zealand's history, Jim, the lad from Taranaki, became the country's 35th Prime Minister at 55 years of age – a role he retained for three consecutive terms (1990-1997). Jim retired as the MP for the Taranaki-King Country in 1998. At the time he'd been the Leader of the National Party for almost 12 years.

Much has been written about Jim's political career, more than we can do justice to in a short cameo story such as this. To learn more, see *"Bolger: A View from the Top"*, written by Jim, *"The Bolger Years, 1990-1997"*, by Margaret Clark, and *"Fridays with Jim: Conversations about our country with Jim Bolger"*, written with David Cohen (these books are available from local and online bookstores).

During this period of their lives, Jim and Joan received numerous honours and awards including the New Zealand 1990 Commemoration Medal to celebrate the 150th anniversary of the signing of the Treaty of Waitangi. In 1998 New Year Honours Jim was appointed a Member of the Order of New Zealand, NZ's highest award, and Joan was appointed a Companion of the New Zealand Order of Merit in recognition for their services to the Crown and to the nation.

What is evident is that Jim and Joan are partners in life. Their relationship and decisions are firmly based on an unwavering shared set of values. Joan accompanied Jim and supported her husband and the constituents he represented, throughout and beyond his political career. Together they managed their farming businesses and have jointly raised their nine children. Jim readily admits that given his responsibilities, he was unable to be at all of their school and sports events. Likewise, Joan accompanied Jim at state engagements and functions both in New Zealand and on overseas trips whenever she could.

In 1998, Jim and Joan began a whole new chapter of their lives when he took on another leadership position – this time as New Zealand's Ambassador to the United States. The role was based in Washington D.C. and the USA became home for Jim, Joan and their two youngest sons for nearly the next four years. In his new role Jim's major responsibility was to continue to strengthen New Zealand - US relations, just as he had when he was Prime Minister after the rupture that occurred when NZ went nuclear free. It was also an occasion to engage with Ambassadors from many countries to discuss foreign policies and promote mutually beneficial relationships with New Zealand. During this period Jim and Joan attended numerous official functions and made many new friends with whom they still keep in contact. These were interesting times.

Jim and Joan with Bill and Hilary and Clinton at the White House

When Jim and Joan arrived in Washington, Bill Clinton was the President and Jim knew him from earlier contacts. In 2001, Bill Clinton was succeeded by George W. Bush as President, whom Jim also knew from earlier contacts.

Unbelievably, one ordinary day, September 11th, 2001, terrorists struck in the heart of America, and the Bolgers were right on hand as those tragic events unfolded. Jim was at a breakfast meeting in downtown Washington when the news came through of the al-Qaeda terrorist attacks. Two of the high-jacked planes crashed into the North and South Towers of the World Trade Centre complex in New York. A third hijacked plane crashed into the Pentagon, the headquarters of the US Department of Defence, only seven miles from Washington DC. A fourth plane, which was understood to be heading for the Capitol, crashed in Pennsylvania after an attempt by the passengers to take control. The impact was global. People around the world watched in horror as these events were televised. Chaos ensued. Nearly three thousand people were killed – some jumping to their deaths as the towers collapsed. Thousands more were injured. Most of those who perished were civilians and more than 90 countries, including New Zealand, lost citizens.

Following the attacks, the Australian and New Zealand Embassies organised an interdenominational service in the church closest to Ground Zero in New York. Jim, as New Zealand's Ambassador to the US, spoke to the gathering and read a letter from Helen Clark, the Prime Minister, expressing "our nation's deepest sympathy to those devastated by the attack". As a result of these terrorist attacks, much stricter travel security measures have been implemented around the globe.

Jim and Joan enjoyed their time in the United States. They visited virtually every state including Alaska and participated in intense and momentous events. As a former Prime Minister Jim received many speaking invitations across the US. They were interesting times across the world and given the major role the US plays Washington was an interesting place. Nevertheless, the Bolgers were happy to return home to New Zealand in early 2002.

At 66 years of age, Jim wasn't ready to retire. He was, and still is, an articulate speaker and inquisitive. He always does his homework. Jim was never afraid to tackle the big issues. He embraces change and to this day is very comfortable in leadership positions. He subsequently accepted numerous leadership roles, for example he was the first Chairman of the Board for Kiwibank, to give the new bank credibility. Jim became the Chair of NZ Post and Express Couriers Ltd. and was Chair of the International Advisory Board of the World Agricultural Forum and the New Zealand United States Council. He currently chairs the Gas Industry Company, which regulates the gas industry and will have a complex role to play as NZ moves to 100% renewable energy. He is a Board member of the Te Urewera Board which was established to *speak for the land*, as was agreed when settling Historic Grievances with Tuhoe. The unique approach was adopted that *no one owned the land as it owns itself* and therefore the Te Urewera Board speaks for the land. "Yes unique, but other countries have now adopted similar provisions".

In his early 70's Jim was elected Chancellor of the University of Waikato – a role he held for the next 12 years.

Chancellor of Waikato University 2007-2019

He is also a member of "The Interaction Council" a high-level group of former Presidents and Prime Ministers, who meet to discuss global ethical, scientific, and political matters. Joan finds these meetings fascinating and accompanies Jim whenever possible. In 2019, the group met in Colombia, but the 2020 meeting planned for Malta was postponed as the COVID outbreak curbed all international travel arrangements for the foreseeable future. A key issue that the Interaction Council has discussed at its last two meetings, is what should replace Gross Domestic Product (GDP) as a more inclusive measure of societal progress? Jim notes that, "this is a complex issue but clearly GDP is no longer an adequate measure and will need to be replaced".

When they returned to New Zealand from Washington, Joan and Jim settled back into their Te Kuiti home on the farm. For a while Jim continued to work from there and from an apartment they bought in Wellington. But the time came when the couple decided their house was more suitable for their son Stephen and his family, who were managing and taking over the farm. Jim and Joan made the decision to move to Waikanae where they are actively involved in the community. Joan said, "Waikanae is a great place to live – very friendly. There are good transport options with a regular train service into Wellington. We have easy access to everything we need". The couple, who celebrated their 58th wedding anniversary this year, continue their interest in current affairs, especially the big issues such as climate change, and meeting the needs of the world community in a more equitable manner. Jim says, "it is obscene that according to Oxfam the ten wealthiest people made $540 Billion in the first year of the COVID-19 emergency, while others starved. Clearly new thinking is necessary".

The couple enjoy reading and share a love of gardening. "Joan weeds, and I plant," said Jim. Reflecting on their lives together Jim said, "We are very lucky, we have a very happy life together. We've slowed down a bit but have not altogether retired. My mother was 104 when she died, so I've got good genes. We do what we find interesting and meet our commitments. We've travelled all over the world and met many very interesting people, including Pope John Paul II, and Sir Edmund Hillary". Jim said he was the first Head of Government to visit the South Pole. He considered Dame Whina Cooper and Nelson Mandela as friends. He attended Mandela's inauguration and returned many years later for his funeral. Jim and Joan also met HRH Queen Elizabeth II several times.

Above all else, Joan and Jim are family orientated. "We are very proud of our nine adult children, and we have 18 grandchildren. We see a lot of them, albeit remotely with some family members living overseas during lockdown. They are all highly successful and get on well together and we are very fortunate to have lived a rewarding and interesting life".

Meeting President Mandela after his Inauguration

Jim with Rod Stewart and his wife Rachael Hunter at the Trentham
Racecourse, on Wellington Cup Day January 1994

Thinking of tomorrow and the changes that will bring, the following anonymous quote resonates:

"The Stone Age, which lasted about 2.5 million years- didn't end because of a lack of stones, but because new ideas were superior".

JIM GIBSON

Jim, the youngest of three children, was raised in Rongotai in Wellington. He enjoyed his primary school years at Miramar South and on reflection he realizes how dedicated teaching staff were. "At the time, the depression was just coming to an end, and the Second World War was about to commence. At school, cricket and rugby union were the most common sports activities, and I took part in both sports, although cricket was my first love".

On leaving primary school in 1942, Jim continued his education at Rongotai College, which at the time was a boys' only college. He recalls he enjoyed most subjects, especially chemistry and mathematics. He also appreciated music and it was about this time that he began having piano lessons. Jim enjoyed this for a year or so, before losing interest in practicing as this reduced the time he could spend outdoors joining in his friends' activities. In his formative years, a lot of his recreational time was spent with a small dinghy in Evans Bay and the Marlborough Sounds with his family. "I just loved it on the water. Later I had a kayak and a dinghy, both of which were built by my clever dad". This interest and enjoyment of the sea probably had a big influence when he considered his future career options while he was in the fourth form. Jim said, "There was a strong family connection to the mercantile marine. Two of my uncles had been master mariners and my dad had been a second mate. I left school at the end of my fourth form year to start a seafaring life in the mercantile marine".

In 1946, Jim was lucky to get his first ship as a deck boy on the 4-masted barque S/V 'Pamir'. This ship had been seized as a war prize in 1942 by the New Zealand government from its Finnish owners. "It became manned with New Zealand crews for trading with North America. This ship was totally reliant on the wind during its voyages of approximately two months each way as it had no engines". With a mainmast 180 feet high, and the experience of working in all weather and heights day and night, setting and furling sails, instilled great confidence and seamanship in young Jim. "This stood me in good stead in future employment", said Jim. There is a plaque to this ship's memory at Frank Kitts Park in Wellington.

Jim with a model of the 'Pamir' at the Vista Club in Paraparaumu.
The model is now in the Maritime Union Office in Wellington

Over the next 17 years Jim sailed in a number of steam and motor ships in both foreign and coastal waters. "I had a stint on ships under the U.K. Ensign before sitting my Mates, and later my Master Mariner's certificates. Jim has many memories of his time at sea. Two in particular stand out. In 1951, the New Zealand Seaman's Union supported the New Zealand Watersiders who protested against financial hardships and poor working conditions. Their Union was de-registered by the

Government. It was the largest and most widespread industrial dispute the nation had ever experienced. Jim said, "This was one of the toughest times in my life. We were on strike for five months with no pay"! He also recalls a funny story. "While working as an Able Seaman on the 'Waiana' (with the Union Steam Ship Company of New Zealand), we were docked on the Yarra River at the bottom of Flinders Street in Melbourne. It was a Friday night, and we were loading a circus to bring it to New Zealand. We'd made a ramp and the elephants were being walked onto the ship when all of a sudden, one of them took off up Flinders Street. It caused pandemonium among the late-night shoppers – absolute chaos until it was caught by the people from the circus! It seems funny now when I look back, but it wasn't at the time".

In 1963, after commands in the Anchor Shipping Company ships, Jim came ashore so he could spend more time with his family. "I took on the position as Senior Port Safety Inspector with the NZ Marine Department. In this role I inspected all the ships that came into Wellington Harbour and everything on the wharf. I remember when the first container ship to New Zealand berthed in the harbour on the morning of Saturday 19th June 1971. It was the 'Columbus New Zealand'. As the independent inspector, it was my job to inspect the cargo gear and advise on safety and compliance with Regulations in New Zealand ports. In 1992 I was promoted to Deputy Superintendent of Mercantile Marine, and I retired from the Public Service the following year". After all those years at sea, Jim's on-shore career with the Marine Department spanned 30 years.

In retirement Jim relocated to Levin to care for his elderly mother. When his mum passed away 10 years later, he moved to the Kāpiti Coast so he could be closer to his family in Wellington and much closer to the marina at Mana where his yacht the 'Jane Rhodes' was moored. "At 70 years of age I thought it was time for me to indulge in what I wanted to do, which was to go sailing. I thought this would be a great retirement hobby. I learned how to handle her and cruised all around the sounds often for 2-4 weeks at a time – weather permitting. Sometimes I had shipmates, other times I sailed solo. Favourite sailing destinations included Nelson, the French Pass, Able Tasman, Torrent Bay, Marlborough Sounds, and Durville Island. For ten years I had so much fun on my yacht – but when it got too heavy to handle on my own, I gave it up".

This photo of 'Jane Rhodes' was taken at Chaffers Marina in Wellington

Throughout his life Jim has always been interested in music. Over the years he's amassed a large collection of classical, popular, big band, jazz, and dance CD's. A keen dancer, he was a regular at the Fernleaf at St Andrews's Hall in Wellington for sequence dancing. In later life, Jim joined the Kāpiti Organ Society and, with renewed interest in learning to play, he purchased a Yamaha organ and took a few lessons. He's since upgraded to a Technics which he plays from time to time, purely for his own enjoyment.

Despite having experienced some challenging health issues, Jim remained positive and has made a good recovery. In his 90's, he lives independently and intends to do so for as long as he can. Jim cherishes time with his daughter Jane, four stepchildren, nine step grandchildren, and three great grandchildren.

Jim with his daughter Jane on her wedding day

Jim is a member of Grey Power, Age Concern, Kāpiti Cottage, a men's coffee club and attends the Kāpiti Club when there is live music. He enjoys the activities these groups and clubs provide as it's an opportunity to meet new people, catch up with old friends, learn something new, and have a good laugh. "Sadly, I have had great friendships with many seafarers and yachties but have outlived most of them. Any day is a good day if one of us is here to see it. I don't do stress"!

In closing Jim suggests 'Pamir under the New Zealand Ensign' written by Jack Churchouse makes good reading.

This photo of Jim was taken at a Pamir Association reunion

ANDY HIGHAM

Prior to retiring 37 years ago, Andy enjoyed a long and successful career with the New Zealand Post and Telegraph Department (renamed NZ Post Office in 1959). His career with the Post Office spanned 41 years – amazing by today's standards! He recalls, "I started in Waimate as a Junior Assistant, earning £60 ($120.00) a year, and later I became a Message Boy delivering telegrams and parcels on a bicycle".

Andy on the left in his uniform with his pal Malcolm White in Waimate

"I relocated to Wellington and in the years that followed I worked my way up the ranks to Senior Clerk, and later became a Senior Postmaster. I was exposed to every aspect of the business with much of the training done on-the-job". As a Postman in Wellington, he walked his route to deliver the mail. "In those days, we used to blow our whistles to let people know we were in the neighbourhood, and sometimes we were offered morning tea from the residents on our route"!

Andy gained further experience when he worked at the Public Service Garage in Wellington where the vehicle fleet operation was managed by the Post Office. He recalls, "All but one of the staff were men, including the chauffeurs. They were an interesting bunch of people. The only female employee worked in the office. All the staff had to be able to drive, so I was taught to drive while I was there." For two years, (1955-1957), Andy was a local organiser promoting the 'National Savings Scheme', whereby he encouraged office and factory workers to join this scheme at 3 ½% interest (better than today's interest rate)!

Andy met Patreece (Pat), his future wife while they were both working - Andy at Ngaio Post Office and Pat in the Telegraph Office. "Things were very different back then as all calls had to go through a central system, and that's how we met - over the telephone" he said. Andy also played the organ at St Luke's in Wadestown, and this is where he and his sweetheart got married in 1949.

Andy and Patreece's Wedding Day

Initially the couple set up home in Trentham. They moved to Titahi Bay when this area was being developed. In the years that followed they had seven children – six boys and a girl (three of whom are now super-annuitants themselves)! The family later moved to a four-bedroomed home in Porirua where they lived for 27 years. During this time Andy's career went from strength to strength. After 21 years of service with the Post Office, he was appointed to the role of Postmaster, a position he held in five different places!

"Pat and I, were very proud of our family watching them grow up; schooling results – the good and the bad, getting jobs and having their own families etc. All of our children went to college, which is more than I did. Our youngest son went to university in Wellington and graduated as an Architect. There were no student loans back then"! Like many families Andy and Pat enjoyed their holidays. "There have been many family camps over the years. Otaki Forks was a popular destination in the early days. Everyone brought their own gear with them which included food etc. We liked to camp near a river so the youngsters could splash around! One year a lamb was taken to cook on a spit. The fire was going all day to cook it, so firewood had to be collected. The lamb had to be turned all day by hand by whoever could turn a handle. The lamb was lovely. Great days"! Andy and Pat were on holiday in Te Aroha with his sister and brother-in-law when the Prime Minister Norman Kirk died in August 1974. He said, "we couldn't get anything to eat or drink as everything was closed including the cafes and the pubs. The country was in mourning".

After 41 years of service, Andy retired from the Post Office in December 1983. "At my farewell, which was held on my last day of work at NaeNae Post Office, the Chief Postmaster Wellington, Mr Derek Calver provided an overview of the history of my service. He gave me a written copy along with a pair of cufflinks with the Post Office emblem on them".

Andy's farewell function at Naenae Post Office on his last day of work

In retirement, Andy undertook voluntary work in the community, became the Treasurer for several groups and continued to play the organ in church as well as at dozens of funeral services held throughout the district each year. "I've always had a passion for music. I started playing the piano when I was seven, and it wasn't long before I was playing for the Sunday School I attended".

Andy's life centred around church activities. Captivated by the music played in St Augustine's church in Waimate, he started learning how to play the organ there at 12 years of age. When the regular organist gave up the role, she passed the job on to Andy, and as the church organist he was frequently asked to play the organ at the weddings and funerals.

Andy playing the piano

The organ at St Augustine's

St Augustine's, Waimate (Artist – Eileen Mayo)

Little did he know at the time that he would be playing the organ in churches for the next 70 years! "In retirement I decided it was time for me to put some energy into music. That meant more time for practices and to learn new music etc. I made up my mind to practice at least one or more hours every day. I only had a harmonium at home and a one-manual pipe organ at Saint Anne's church in Porirua. These instruments got a lot of use over a period of time. I have always classed myself as a church organist and being a Recitalist is something different, so I tried to raise my standard a little bit. I revived some pieces that I could play reasonably well and learned some new stuff".

A decade into his retirement, after experiencing some health issues, Andy underwent heart surgery. Over time he made a good recovery, but he and Pat came to the decision that neither of them was getting any younger. It was time to downsize their property to a more manageable level, while at the same time retain their connection and interests in the community. In 2007, after doing their research the couple moved into a sunny villa in a retirement village in Levin. It was a good decision; one they never regretted. They embraced life in the village and also participated in activities outside the village. Andy became a volunteer with the Levin Budget Service and the Levin Music Society, and he continued to play the organ in church and at the funeral parlours until he was 82 years old. Even then he kept his harmonium at home for a number of years before he finally decided it was time to get rid of it.

Family has always been important to Andy and Pat. Their seven children grew up and had families of their own. "Altogether we have 18 grandchildren and 15 great grandchildren, and most of the family live in New Zealand". Over the years he and his wife celebrated so many special occasions together including their 25th, 50th and 60th Wedding Anniversaries. For Andy's 90th birthday party, the family gathered at a holiday park in Paekakariki for a long weekend to enjoy this special time together. Andy said, "we keep records of all of these do's". These records and photos are a family treasure.

Andy and Patreece's Golden Wedding Anniversary

Another milestone was the couple's 60th wedding anniversary. "Looking back on these photos, the young folk look so young. We renewed our wedding vows at the church where we were married, Saint Luke's Anglican Church in Wadestown.

Andy and Patreece renewing their vows with Rev. Tric Malcolm
"Those whom God hath joined together, let no man put asunder".

All of our immediate family turned up, plus a few friends". "The organist played 'Jesu, joy of man's desiring' during the communion. More photos were taken. We had three albums produced for the 60th. We got lots and lots of cards from all and sundry, including the Queen"!

"When the local newspaper heard of our celebrations, they interviewed us and took a photo, and this appeared in the Levin Chronicle (4 September 2009), with the article titled 'A marriage full of highlights'".

"Granddaughter Gemma Higham, centre, helps celebrate
Andy and Pat Higham's 60th wedding anniversary"

Sadly, Patreece died in January 2018. The couple had been happily married for nearly 70 years. Andy still lives in the villa they shared together surrounded by a friendly, supportive community within the village. He said, "Now I'm 94, it's hard to believe I've been retired for 37 years – nearly as long as I was employed in the workforce. I take every day as it comes. It's easy to live here in the village. There is no stress and no worries. I join in the village activities that interest me and I do what I want to do outside the village. During the COVID lockdown I got my groceries through the Summerset system and my seven children kept in regular contact with me over the phone. Since the lockdown restrictions have been lifted, we have resumed the companionship we have always enjoyed over a game of cards and at happy hour".

Living independently Andy has a very positive outlook on life. In his 95th year, encouraged by his adult children, he's been busy capturing his memories as a legacy project for his family and friends. It's a precious gift few families have and will be truly treasured.

This is one of Andy's favourite quotes:

"We make a living by what we get, we make a life by what we give" **– Winston Churchill.**

A Prayer For Those Of Us In Later Years
from the writings of a 17th Century Nun

Dear Lord,

You know that I am getting old. Please keep me from the habit of thinking I must say something on every subject on every occasion.

Release me from the craving to straighten out everybody's affairs.

Make me thoughtful but not moody; helpful but not bossy.

Keep me from the recital of endless details; give me wings to get to the point.

Lord, seal my lips on my aches and pains, they are increasing, and love of rehearsing them is becoming sweeter by the day,

Help me to endure the tales of others' pains, and grant humility when my memory seems to clash with the memory of others.

Teach me the lesson that sometimes I may be mistaken.

Father, give me the ability to see good things in unexpected places, and talents in unexpected people, and give me the grace O Lord, to tell them so.

Amen

JEAN DOUGLAS

Major life changing decisions can be difficult to make for most people and can have significant consequences. Jean, though, now in her 90's, has always been open to opportunities and has never been afraid to make them. An independent woman, she moved to New Zealand in her 70's to begin the next chapter in her life and proudly became a citizen four years later. "I'd visited my cousin in New Zealand the year before. While here, I toured the South Island and had the amazing experience of swimming with the dolphins in Akaroa Harbour. The captain of the boat said he'd never seen so many dolphins at one time and they'd never stayed so long before". For Jean it was a defining moment – "I promised myself I would come here to live".

Returning to her home on the Isle of Wight in the English Channel, she sold her holiday business, packed up her belongings, and "using my English bull-dog tenacity" worked with the authorities to complete all of the immigration requirements. It's a decision she has never regretted.

Jean was born in Rochester in Kent in 1927. The second of two children, her brother Harold was 17 years older, and as the age gap was so big, the siblings didn't spend much time together. Tragically, her mother died when she was two, and although her mother's, sister stepped in and lovingly helped to raise Jean, she too died when Jean was only seven.

Experiencing a sense of abandonment, Jean was a vulnerable child and was emotionally and physically abused by the people who were 'caring' for her. Unsurprisingly, her childhood memories are not all happy ones. Jean said, "Since then, I have spent my life searching for knowledge and understanding of who I am". A spiritual person, she looks for the beauty and good in the physical world.

A treasured photo of Jean's mother

Jean approximately 8 years old at Langford, Essex

Growing up during the Second World War Jean distinctly remembers, "how scary it was when 33 German planes flew overhead to firebomb London". When she turned 16, she moved to Coventry to live with her brother and while there, the city was bombed. During this time, she worked as a volunteer on air force bases in Worcester but was discharged when the authorities discovered she was underage. Her first paid job was with the General Post Office (GPO), in the division that was later known as British Telecom (BT).

Just after the war ended, Jean married her sweetheart Maurice Ley who was conscripted in the Army. The couple's first child, Julie-Ann was born in 1947, and their second child, Nigel John was born in 1952. When Maurice was demobbed, the couple owned and operated a Butcher business in Kent. "Maurice was a butcher. He loved his trade and he put his all into the business. He taught me how to bone meat and make sausages and brawn. We lived on the premises – the house was built in 1286. While he worked in the shop, I delivered the meat to our customers throughout the district".

The Family Butcher's Shop

While raising their family Jean became interested in alternative medicine. She trained in Massage, Remedial Massage, and Reflexology. Jean said, "I've always been a spiritual person. I believe that we are all born with the energy". Furthering her studies, she enrolled at the Arthur Findley Psychic College for

Spiritual Advancement and was especially interested in spiritualist healing and awareness. Travelling to Lincolnshire, she trained to the intermediate teaching level in the Aura Soma healing system, designed to work with the mind, body, and spirit as a whole with colours, crystals, magnets, and sound. She was a member of the Federation of Healing for 14 years and became a Numerologist. Jean, who had always been artistic and enjoyed painting, began writing a collection of poems and decorated each one with a flourish of hand painted designs. These are all interests she maintains to this day.

As time passed, the children were growing up. Maurice was heavily involved with the business he enjoyed – it was his life. But Jean wanted more. "He was a wonderful husband and although we really cared for one another and loved our children, we mutually agreed to part ways".

Following the separation, Jean secured work with her GPO training. She also managed a Post Office and gift shop with a friend for a short time. Chance meetings happen to all of us in life, and one such occasion stands out for Jean. "I had major surgery at London Hospital. On the very last day I was there, I joined a gentleman at the only table with a vacant chair and we spoke for the first time". The couple became good friends and from that day on, they kept in touch with one another. Over time the relationship blossomed. Jean later moved to the Isle of Wight to care for her friend Bob as he was terminally ill. "One of his last three wishes was to marry me, and I agreed". The wedding went ahead, but sadly Bob died four days later. After his untimely death, Jean decided to stay on the Isle of Wight. She bought a holiday business which she ran for the next 23 years.

The brochure advertising Jean's holiday business

The climate on the island with its seaside holiday feel really suited Jean, and she enjoyed swimming at the beach in her spare time. In this atmosphere Jean's creative energy flourished. Using acrylics and watercolours, her range of artwork included, birds, flowers, portraits, landscapes, and a series of butterfly paintings, which were later made into gift cards. She also wrote a collection of more than 50 poems.

Jean's children, who both lived in the UK often asked her when she was going to retire – but she had no plans to do so. As described earlier, Jean's life changed direction after visiting a cousin in New Zealand. Without hesitation she sold her business, migrated to Aotearoa, and bought a home in a retirement village on the Kāpiti Coast. Jean enjoys living in close proximity to the sea and activities associated with it. She has a particular interest in the 'Round The World Yacht Race' and had taken photos of the yacht races while on the Isle of Wight. When the BT Global Challenge yacht was moored in Wellington Harbour, she went along to see it. She met the captain and showed him the photos. Recalling the event she said, "The vessels were unable to sail from Yarmouth as there was no wind. Everyone had gone home. I was at the Needles and after a while the wind began to blow. Luckily, I had my camera with me and was able to capture the moment others had missed. It was incredibly exciting. The captain was so thrilled to see the photos he took copies. Then he invited me onboard to have my photo taken"!

Jean aboard the BT Global Challenge yacht in Wellington Harbour

As a psychic artist Jean continued her spirituality training in New Zealand and in Australia and appreciates the gift of healing through her hands, she has been given. Jean recalls, "One morning in 2004, I was woken with a voice that said, 'get a pen and write'. My guide's name is White Buffalo - an American Cheyenne Indian. He channels messages of love, respect and peace for all the people of the Universe, no matter what their colour or creed".

Channeling is known as a natural form of communication between people and spirits. In the years since that first experience with White Buffalo, Jean has documented 287 spiritual messages from him (for more information see whitebuffalo.co.nz).

Jean's spiritual photo, and her painting of White Buffalo

Jean's son Nigel, (who was Rupert Murdoch's chauffeur for more than a decade), regularly visited his mother in New Zealand. Heartbreakingly, both he and Jean's daughter Julie-Ann died within months of one another in 2006 – both of cancer. Words can't describe how devasting this was for Jean, especially being so far away from her grandchildren and great-grandchildren during this difficult period. Following the loss of her children, Jean's health rapidly deteriorated. She developed peripheral neuropathy - nerve damage resulting in numbness and sharp pains in her hands and feet. Despite her physical limitations, Jean who is now in her mid-90's, still lives independently. She has a very positive outlook on life, is quick-witted, has a sharp mind, and focuses on what she can do in life. She is very interested in current affairs, enjoys a debate, but she tries not to get bogged down in the negative news articles that are widely distributed to the public. In her words "there is beauty everywhere if you open your eyes to see it, and there is beauty in everything we speak when we find the right energy".

To this day Jean still writes poems. To celebrate the late Lady

Diana Spencer's 60th birthday celebration Jean sent a copy of a poem entitled 'The Queen of Hearts' to Earl Charles Spencer in England, and he kindly wrote back to thank her.

Jean with the Thank You card from Earl Charles Spencer and one of her butterfly notecards

She has donated the electronic copy of her collection of beautiful butterfly notecards to Starship Hospital so that they can produce them for themselves, (to use or sell), to help contribute to the funds for the hospital.

A practical person, she has planned her funeral arrangements – but isn't planning to implement them any time soon! The following photograph appears on the back page of her funeral service sheet she said, "If everyone doesn't leave laughing, it won't be my fault"!

JUNE ROWLAND

June was born in Wellington in 1924 and grew up in Rongotai in the eastern suburbs of the city. She went to Miramar South Primary School and then on to Wellington East Girls College where she completed her secondary education. During the war years she worked at the Bank of New Zealand. In 1947, June married her fiancé Fred Rowland who had recently been demobbed after six years' service in the New Zealand Army. The newlyweds shared a love of the outdoors and in 1948, shortly after they married, they moved 52 kilometres up the coast to Raumati which was mostly all farmland at the time. The couple bought a section for £175 in an early subdivision that had no services or amenities and looked forward to building a home of their own. Initially they lived in a rented bach that had a long-drop toilet and no bathroom or laundry – it was quite different to what they had been used to in the city. Nevertheless, Fred set to work to build them a home of their own and they started a family.

June and Fred's house in Miro Road, was the first house to be built in the street. June said, "when we moved in, it had no fences. We had no power - no electricity for nine months. I boiled water on a primus and had a two-burner kerosene stove to cook on. I used a copper that was fueled by a wood fire to do the washing. We had a tank on a stand to collect rainwater from the roof, septic tanks and soak pits took care of sewage and wastewater and there was no rubbish collection service". By this time, their son John was just a toddler and June also cared for Christine their newborn baby, so life wouldn't have been easy. Within three years the family expanded with the arrival of their third child Sandra.

Like most mothers at the time, June stayed home to look after the children. She established a garden, and while the children were growing up, she developed a lifelong interest and awareness of her surroundings in this predominantly rural area. June had always been interested in the environment. As a teenager she enjoyed the bush and had been a member of the Tararua Tramping Club. She took up this activity again in the Kāpiti district and became a founding member of the Parawai Tramping Club. The children also enjoyed life outdoors. Her son John later became actively involved in hunting, mountain biking and tramping. Her daughters Christine and Sandra belonged to the Kāpiti Pony Club and, as they grew up, became keen trampers.

During these years there was virtually no part-time work in the area. Consequently, there were limited opportunities for homemakers to earn money of their own to supplement the family's budget. When June and five of her friends became aware of a Hutt Valley business that was looking for outworkers to assemble hair rollers, they were all very keen to give it a go. To get the contract the women had to form a company and agree to a quota. What initially seemed impossible, became a reality, when the 'curler girls' set up the "Raumati Assembly Company". They sourced premises, (an old Army hut), where they could store their bulk supplies and meet to assemble and pack the rollers. For the next decade, the women successfully ran this business and always delivered on their quota! Recalling these days June said, "We did this work around our family commitments and had lots of laughs when we got together. When we fulfilled the quota, we'd phone the guy up on the party line and he'd send a truck to come and take it all away". One of the industrious women in this group was June Oakley who became the district's first female Mayor" (1980-1983)!

When her children grew up June became involved with the Parawai Tramping Club. In her late 40's she planned and coordinated tramping trips and helped raise funds to purchase a truck to transport people. A few years later a Council Recreation Officer asked June to lead a walk; "I planned a day's walk in the Maungakotukutuku Ranges that was held on a weekend. On the day 20 people came along, but the weather was awful. It was very wet, and the track was slippery. I thought none of them would want to go tramping again, but at the end of the day, one of the people in the group said they'd enjoyed it so much they wanted to do this again, and the others all agreed"! Encouraged by the response June and her friend Jan Nisbet set up a group for retired people called 'Kāpiti Weekday Walkers' – by this time June was 59 years of age, but chronological age is no barrier to enjoying the outdoors with like-minded individuals. This group is still operating very successfully under different leadership. Reflecting back on her tramping experience June said, "Approaching 60 years of age, I didn't think I should be doing this anymore, after all, 60 was considered to be quite old in those days, but it's quite different these days".

When Fred retired, he also became more involved in tramping. June said, "He was a good leader and a fit man. Every week we did a day's walk. We'd charge people between two and four dollars to cover car-pooling expenses to get to and from the local tracks. People just loved meeting and talking to one another. Tramping is not only a healthy and uplifting experience, it's a very social way of meeting people and connecting with and appreciating the environment". Fred and June also organised trips further afield to places like Ruapehu, Waikaremoana, Hanmer Springs and the Nelson Lakes. Each year they chose different locations for these longer walks so people could explore, experience, and appreciate the native bush and natural scenery in both the North and the South Island of New Zealand.

In the late 1970's and early 80's June attended university extension courses in the evenings in Wellington. She studied botany and geology and, as she became aware of feminism and women's issues, she enrolled in women's studies. "I joined the local branch of the 'Women's Electoral Lobby' (WEL). We contributed to the National WEL newsletter and made several submissions to suggested by-laws concerning women on such things as abortion rights, pornography, snuff movies and equal pay. Members spoke at Select Committee meetings. These were interesting and rewarding years and helped me realise that women can change the perception of government thinking". Around this time, with a growing awareness of a nuclear threat, June also belonged to an anti-nuclear group.

In her late 50's, June developed an interest in solo parents when she became aware of the loneliness and isolation experienced by young women in this situation. Encouraged by a Recreational Officer who worked at the Kāpiti Coast District Council, June set up a group for solo parents where they could come together with their babies in a supportive environment. She said, "in the late 70's early 1980's it wasn't easy to get the support that was needed for these young women". Nevertheless, June hired the Scout Hall at Paraparaumu Beach and spread the word in the community to encourage solo parents to come together to support one another.

Hearing about a similar group that was operating in Wellington, June went along to their meetings and with their support she started a group for young mothers in Raumati called the 'New Mothers Support Group'. Four years later, as more young mothers became involved, June was able to step back from her role as they took responsibility for running the structured development programme for themselves.

At 61 years of age, June became a member of the Queen Elizabeth Park Board in Paekakariki. The 1,580 acre park on the Kāpiti Coast, with its natural dunes and coastal walkways is a place of historical significance for local Maori and the US Marines who camped there during the war. The park was opened in 1953 when the Queen visited New Zealand. Over the years the recreational facilities have been developed and it is now home to the Wellington Tramway Museum. At 67, years of age, instead of slowing down, June took on more responsibility when she became a member of the Wellington Conservation Board – a role she held for three years. The Board covered all of the Wellington Conservancy including the Hutt Valley, West Coast, the Wairarapa and the Tararua District.

Reflecting back on her life June said, "I became concerned about the escalating number of new sub-divisions that Council was approving in the area with seemingly little interest in preserving our environment. We were losing our native bush, our wetlands and birdlife, and our coastal landscape was rapidly eroding. With the introduction of the Resource Management Act almost all environmental policy-making and management was devolved to regional and local Councils - but they were unaware of the environmental impact of their decisions". As a consequence, June started up the Kāpiti Environmental Action Inc. (KEA) in 1990 with like-minded long-term Kāpiti residents.

KEA established a set of principles to guide their actions and decisions. Seven core action groups were set up to address their concerns. June led the 'Forests Reserves and Wetlands action group', and later became the Chairperson of KEA. They established quarterly public meetings and invited representatives from the various government agencies to discuss their concerns. As developers applied to Council to subdivide land, KEA submitted objections and suggestions. June said, "We did our research, and consulted with everyone including council officers, developers, representatives from government agencies, lawyers, the local iwi and members of the community. We prepared submissions, ran campaigns, held public meetings in the community and distributed a regular newsletter. As a team we discovered we had skills and expertise we were previously unaware of".

KEA challenged the Council on the impact of their decisions which focused on the income generated at the expense of the natural features of our environment. June said, "We were talking about coastal erosion and the loss of our wetlands, in retrospect we were talking about climate change". KEA Inc. took Kāpiti District Council to the Environment Court seven times and won six of these cases. Recalling these events June said, "It was amazing what we achieved. I had never spoken in public before, so I was really stretched to do this, but I learned. I was so strongly committed to protecting and preserving our environment that it became easy to speak about it. The

Department of Conservation provided advice and we sought legal advice from a Wellington firm of lawyers. Over time we gained credibility to the extent that we could influence the decision makers".

In recognition for her dedication to the preservation of the landscape, wetlands, and remnants of the forest on the Kāpiti Coast, June was awarded the New Zealand Commemoration Medal, also known as the Sesquicentennial Award. The New Zealand Department of Conservation also presented June with the "Conservation Week Award for Protection of Special Landscapes".

Left, June's New Zealand 1990 Commemoration Medal.
Right June's Conservation Week Award for Protection of Special
Landscapes

Two years later she was awarded the Queens Service Medal "in recognition of her tireless work for the Kāpiti Coast community".

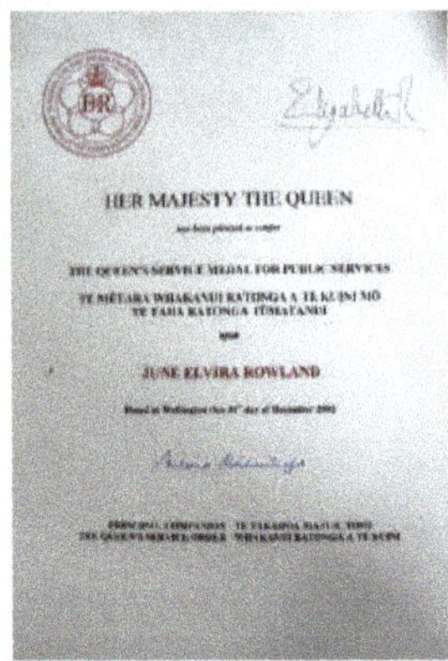

June's Queens Service Medal for Public Service

KEA Inc. disbanded in 2008 when three of the core group retired. By this time June was 84 years old. Following the idea being suggested by Kāpiti Coast District Council, and with their financial support, June and Daphne Steele, who was also a founder member of KEA, have captured the story of this incredible group of people in the book 'The work of KEA – Kāpiti Environment Action Inc.' Looking back over the years with KEA June said, "It was a wonderful learning experience and I met so many interesting and talented people from all walks of life". As some developers appealed a decision to a higher court, some cases took five or six years to resolve. As a result, the following phrase was coined, "KEA Keeps on Keeping On"!

In 2018, with the support of family and friends June wrote "Early Years in Miro Road, Raumati, Paraparaumu". This is a personal and historical account of how this area was established and developed in the 1950's and 60's and captures the context and the memories of the daily life of the families in Miro Road during this period. As previously noted, June and Fred Rowland were the first to build their house in Miro Road. June, who at the time of writing was 96 years of age, still lived there.

June feels very fortunate that her three adult children, five grandchildren and eight great grandchildren all live in the North Island, so she is able to spend time with them. Reflecting on her life June said, "apart from raising my family, most of my achievements have occurred since I turned 50". It's important to note that during these years June also cared for her elderly parents, who lived close by. Her mother lived until she was nearly 102 years old! June said, "it's been an incredibly fulfilling life", which just goes to show that,

"People are capable, at any time in their lives, of doing what they dream of" - Paul Coehlo.

June and Fred planting Kahikatea in the Dell at Whareroa Farm Reserve in 2009.

June Rowland

AFTERTHOUGHTS

It's been a privilege to have chatted with so many interesting men and women who generously shared their stories with me. It's with their permission that a lifetime of wildly different backgrounds, experiences and perspectives can be shared with you. In the second half of life all of these individuals live in New Zealand. Some are single, have partners, are married, or are widowed – just like us. Whilst the physiological aspects of ageing varied from person to person, life for these individuals is a continuous adventure. They proactively pursue activities that interest them, maintain their physical and mental health and wellbeing, and are connected to the community in which they live. It's evident that life holds seasons of change for everyone, things do not always go the way we wish. Despite the unique set of circumstances and challenges these men and women have encountered, they focus their energy on what's within their control, and continually stretch themselves to create their reality.

Chronological age for these individuals is just a number – not an impediment. They challenge the stereotypical belief that advancing age narrows down life choices. They move out of their comfort zones to take on new challenges, learn new skills and take calculated risks. They are resilient. They appreciate that their experiences, and the lessons they have learned along the way, have shaped who they are and the choices they make. Their attitudes to life and their perspective on ageing is both insightful and inspirational. They create life and all that it offers on their own terms, and inspired by their example, so can we!

It's never too late to change direction, start something new, live in a different place, make bold decisions, take on significant projects and invest in meaningful relationships. It's up to each of us to make the most of our extended lifespans. After all, life truly is a gift for us to enjoy, and later life can be even more fulfilling than what has gone before.

Go well and enjoy the adventure – **Angela Robertson**

THANK YOU

Thank you for reading **Creating Life On Our Own Terms**. I hope you enjoyed it. I'd really appreciate it if you would take a few minutes to provide a review of this book, whether positive or negative as reviews help other readers find books that would be of interest to them.

By the same author

Available online from your favourite bookstores

Coming soon
Retirement Reinvented
and
Entrepreneurs @ 50+ - Yes, We Can!

Want to be kept up-to-date with new books and news?

If so, email me to register your interest and be one of the first to find out when new books are released.

Kiaora@angelarobertson.nz

ABOUT THE AUTHOR

Dr Angela Robertson has over 30 years' experience as a professional learning and development practitioner, manager, coach, writer and speaker. She inspires and supports individuals of all ages to maximise their potential to enhance the quality of their lives, work and relationships.

Angela lives with her husband Bill on the beautiful Kāpiti Coast in New Zealand.

www.AngelaRobertson.nz

Angela Robertson Maximising Potential/Facebook